OLD UTAH
T R A I L S

When the hand of the Creator swept across this land we call Utah, it did so with elegance and grace, and endowed us with a gift of exquisite beauty.

The Utah Geographic Series is a celebration of this vast landscape that stretches for 85,000 square miles across the state of Utah. The Series will portray in words and photographs the unique diversity of Utah's astounding landforms, colorful history, expansive natural areas and vigorous people.

It is our hope that through the Series, Utahns and visitors alike will develop a deeper understanding and appreciation of the wonder that is Utah.

Rick Reese
Publisher

Autumn in the La Sal Mountains. The Spanish Trail entered Utah just south of the La Sals.
Jeff Gnass

OLD UTAH
TRAILS

WILLIAM B. SMART

UTAH GEOGRAPHIC SERIES, INC.

SALT LAKE CITY, UTAH

1988

INTRODUCTION

On the desk before me is a page torn from some magazine or other. There's a map of the American West, with red lines— forty-four of them—spider-webbing out from a hub at the southern end of Great Salt Lake toward destinations like Los Angeles, San Francisco, Portland, Anchorage, Calgary, Minneapolis, New York, St. Louis, Atlanta, Jacksonville, Dallas, and Phoenix. Bold letters proclaim *"Salt Lake—Center of the West . . . 368 flights and 44,000 seats every day . . . 10,000 hotel rooms . . . 675,000 sq. ft. convention center . . . "*

Beside this Salt Lake Convention and Visitors Bureau ad lie two other maps. One, the official Utah highway map, shows the heavy green lines of Interstates 15 and 80 stretching to the four points of the compass from Salt Lake Valley. The other, published by the state in 1948, shows a bewildering network of historic trails radiating out from the same hub.

So it is no mere hyperbole, the slogan used by Utah promoters and by the Mormon Tabernacle Choir for half a century— *"Cross-roads of the West."*

This is, and has been, the crossroads. No place else in the West has seen such a convergence of travel or of the historic events associated with it. Consider:

In his abortive attempt to forge a trail from Santa Fe to California, Escalante swung far north because he wanted to reach Utah Lake. Jedediah Smith, who ranged over more of the West than any other man, called Great Salt Lake his *"home in the West"*. The rendezvous system that pulled in trappers from hundreds of miles around centered in the

mountain valleys of northern Utah and southwest Wyoming. The switch that connected the nation by telegraph in 1860 was thrown on Salt Lake City's Main Street. The spike that connected the nation by rail in 1869 was driven seventy-five miles to the north. Salt Lake was a major destination of the Lincoln Highway, in 1913 the first to cross the nation, and of the Arrowhead Highway, completed in 1916 from Los Angeles. The first airmail flew into Salt Lake City in April 1936, and the first airline passenger flew out of there a few days later.

This book is a celebration of those men and women who looked to the far horizons and had the imagination, fortitude, and strength to get there. It is a celebration, too, of the land through which they traveled— this diverse and wondrous land of Utah with its red rock canyons and mesas, vast desert valleys, streams bubbling through alpine meadows, foaming down deep-carved canyons, and losing themselves in the salt lakes or sand and alkali playas of the Great Basin.

The history of the trails provides endless fascination to those attuned to the past. The land across which the trails pass brings renewal to those who find in mountains and deserts relief from the pressures of the modern world.

There are gaps in this book. Most glaring is the absence of a chapter on John C. Fremont. He was a towering figure. Through his expeditions of 1843, '44, '45 and again in 1853-4, he did more than any pre-settlement man to map and describe the trails of what is now Utah. But for a man known

to the nation as The Pathfinder, he found precious few paths in this area. He made, in 1845, the first known crossing of the Salt Desert and gave Pilot Peak its name, but the rest of his exploring mostly followed tracks made by others. In 1843 he traveled over South Pass on what would become the Oregon-California trail, but Jedediah Smith had opened that trail in 1824. He explored the Great Salt Lake, but Jim Clyman had spent twenty-four days circumnavigating it eighteen years earlier. He set out across the Great Basin in search of a mythical river, but Jedediah Smith had proved its non-existence eighteen years before. He crossed the Uintah Basin in 1844, but General William Ashley had done it in 1825. He traversed most of Utah north to south and back in 1844 and 1854, but Smith had done it in 1826 and '27, and the dust had long been deep on the Old Spanish Trail that Fremont followed much of the way. So with due respect to one of the truly great figures in the opening of the West, Fremont will not be included in this volume.

There are other omissions—men like Lieutenant Edward Beckwith and Captain J. H. Simpson, whose explorations in the 1850s helped establish the route of the Pony Express and, later, the Lincoln Highway through the west Utah desert. But much of their work retraced steps made earlier by the Mormon scout and settler, Howard Egan. There was Peter Skene Ogden, a Hudson's Bay Company brigade leader, who in 1828 and '29 made what may have been the first tracks to the north of Great Salt Lake, but his route is too uncertain to describe. And there was Captain Howard Stansbury whose 1849 survey of the Great Salt Lake took him around the west edge of the salt flats. He came back across the flats in the Donner tracks, and left no other trail of his own.

Another omission: The Union Pacific-Central Pacific railroad race across Utah that left 100 miles of graded right of way stretching side by side through the desert before the 1869 wedding of the rails at Promontory. A trip over those long-abandoned gradings—given plenty of time and good shock absorbers—is a stirring reminder of the battle between Irish and Chinese work gangs to see which of the railroad giants could lay the most track and grab the biggest share of the government's subsidy.

And there's the Lincoln Highway, that ambitious effort of early automobile and tire companies to get the nation out of the mud with the first transcontinental highway. A national scandal raged over Utah's failure to fulfill its contract to build the highway through the west desert along the old Pony Express route. That route would have made Ely, Nevada the point of dividing the highways to Los Angeles and San Francisco. Utah's power structure wanted that division to be at Salt Lake City, so instead built what would be Highway 40 across the Salt Flats to Wendover. Nevada's effort to build its section of the Lincoln Highway to Ely was largely wasted. Utah's section is long forgotten.

Those and other stories should be told. But for this volume, the line had to be drawn somewhere.

What, then, is this book? Rather, what is it not?

It's not a trail guide. I have tried to be descriptive enough that, with the excellent maps (done under the direction of Brian Haslam at the University of Utah), the trails can be generally followed. To follow them closely, more is needed, but for many, regrettably, not much more is available. In the back of the book I have listed a few sources that will be helpful, but I have not attempted to provide a comprehensive bibliography. Some of the sources cited are out of print and scarce. More work is needed if the trails are going to stay alive for our children.

Nor can this book be called a work of historical scholarship. I have drawn heavily on original diaries, journals, and reminiscences brought together by the historians listed later, and gratefully acknowledge my debt to them.

Perhaps the book is best described as a personal celebration of the past and the land. It grows from many years of exploring the remote places of Utah, and from growing respect and admiration for the men and women who reached those places through hardship and danger that are difficult to imagine. Not every foot of every trail have I now hiked or driven, but close. And what inspiring and entertaining travel companions I found the Spanish padres, Jedediah Smith, Orson Pratt, Jefferson Hunt, Platte Lyman and others to be.

There have been other choice companions on the trail. Grant Williams and the late Arnold R. Standing of the Forest Service

taught me, during countless hours in the saddle, to see the land as the Mountain Men may have seen it. Lynn Lyman of Blanding, four-wheeler extraordinaire, showed me the Hole-in-the-Rock trail in a way only possible from a man who has spent much of his eighty years out there and whose father was part of the original expedition. Historian Gregory Crampton, now living and writing in St. George, jeeped over the southwest Utah part of the Spanish Trail with me and generously shared files and knowledge of it and of trails in general; his definitive book in progress on the Spanish Trail is eagerly awaited. Montell Seeley and John Jorgenson, lifelong residents of Castle Valley, took us carefully over the ground covered by the Spanish Trail and Gunnison. Pat Hearty, national president of the Pony Express Association, took time from the annual re-enactment ride to share his love for and knowledge of that trail. Milt Hokanson and Bob Springmeyer helped a gimpy-legged writer down the ice-sheathed Hole-in-the-Rock in mid-January and shared delightful days on other trails. F. A. Barnes has been generous in sharing his research. So have Ward Roylance and LaMont Crabtree and others.

Rick Reese's companionship on the trail and his love of the land and its history brought me into this project. His enthusiasm and encouragement saw me through it.

But most thanks go to my favorite trail companion, Donna. She has hiked and jeeped with me what trails she could, tolerated my absence when she couldn't, encouraged, critiqued, and motivated always.

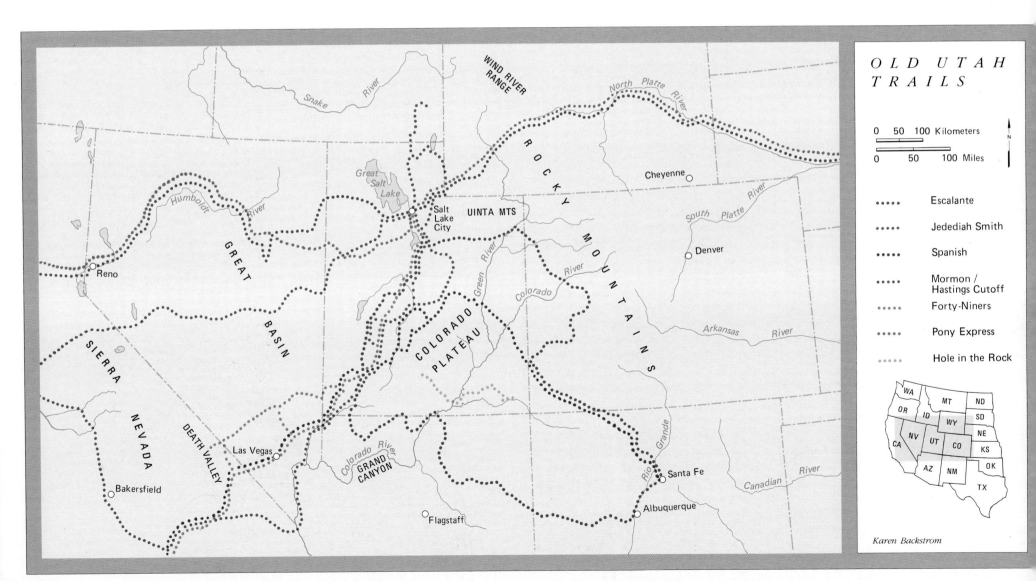

Pine Valley Mountains north of St. George. The Escalante Expedition, Jedediah Smith, travelers on the Spanish Trail and the Forty-Niners passed these mountains.
Stephen Trimble

I. ESCALANTE

Cottonwoods line the Green River through Split Mountain. "The river," *Escalante wrote,* "was the boundary between the Commanche and Ute Indian nations."
John George

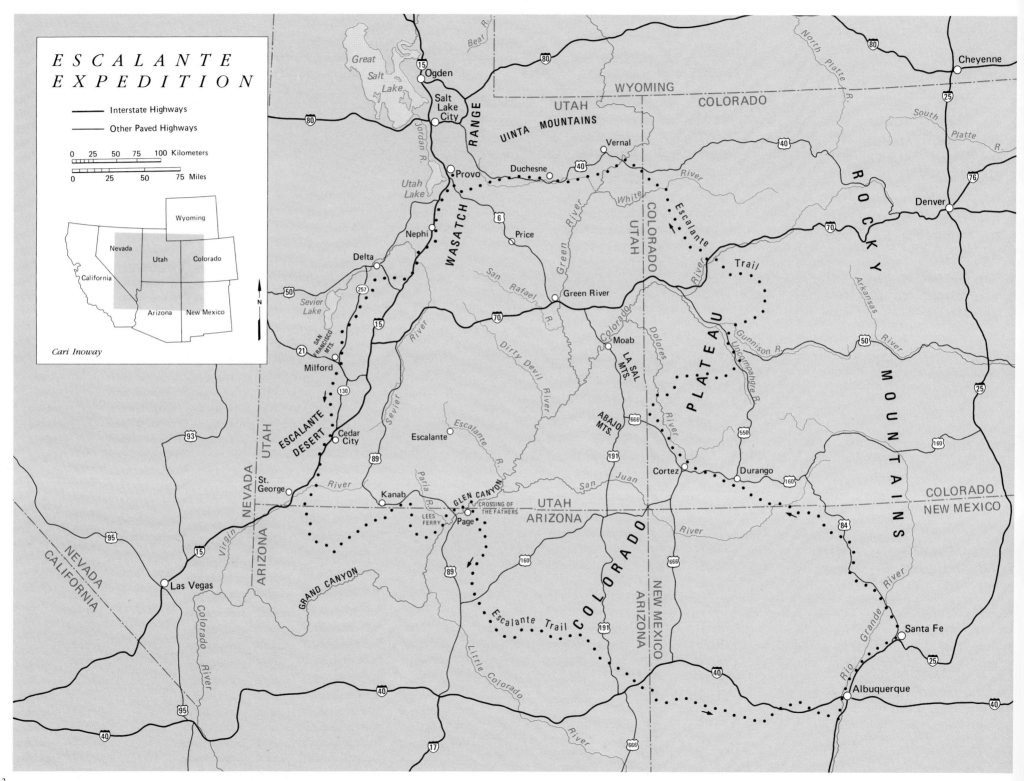

ESCALANTE EXPEDITION

Interstate Highways
Other Paved Highways

0 25 50 75 100 Kilometers

0   25   50   75 Miles

Cari Inoway

Wyoming

Nevada

Utah   Colorado

California

Arizona   New Mexico

N

WYOMING

UTAH   COLORADO

Great Salt Lake

Ogden

Salt Lake City

UINTA MOUNTAINS

Vernal

Duchesne

Provo

Utah Lake

WASATCH RANGE

Price

Green River

Escalante

Trail

ROCKY

Denver

Cheyenne

North Platte R.

South Platte R.

Nephi

Delta

Sevier Lake

SAN FRANCISCO MTS.

Milford

Escalante City

Cedar City

Escalante

Kanab

St. George

Las Vegas

NEVADA
UTAH

ARIZONA

GRAND CANYON

COLORADO River

Virgin River

LEES FERRY

GLEN CANYON

Page

CROSSING OF THE FATHERS

UTAH
ARIZONA

Little Colorado River

Escalante Trail

Green River

San Rafael R.

Dirty Devil River

Sevier River

Escalante R.

Paria R.

Moab

LA SAL MTS.

ABAJO MTS.

Colorado River

Dolores River

San Juan River

COLORADO

Cortez

PLATEAU

Uncompahgre R.

Gunnison R.

Durango

MOUNTAINS

Arkansas River

COLORADO
NEW MEXICO

NEW MEXICO
ARIZONA

Rio Grande River

Santa Fe

Albuquerque

MOUNTAINS

ESCALANTE

In my boyhood eyes, four men stood as giants in the romance of western exploration. Two of them, Meriwether Lewis and William Clark, did their pathfinding to the Pacific Coast far to the north of Utah's borders and have no place in this volume. The third was Jedediah Smith, of whom more later.

The fourth—the first, actually—was Father Silvestre Velez de Escalante.

Maybe it's because he was the first white man known to have set foot on Utah soil that Escalante is such a romantic figure, or because he did it in such a memorable year, 1776. Maybe it's the image of this humble Spanish priest in homespun cassock and skullcap blazing a trail diagonally from one corner to the other of what would become the state of Utah. Maybe it's the drama of his desperate search for a crossing of the Colorado, and that marvelously evocative name he gave a campsite deep in the bowels of Glen Canyon: Salsipuedes—*"Get out if you can."*

Maybe it's the possibility that if his church had heeded Escalante's plea to establish a mission among the Indians on Utah Lake, Utahns today would be speaking Spanish.

Whatever. The image and the romance have never faded. Escalante's diary, one of the finest in all western history, still stirs the blood. So does a retracing of his route, across the windswept wastes of the Uintah Basin, over the Wasatch Mountains at one of the most difficult places he could have found, down the long desert valleys of central Utah, and finally east through the redrock mesas and canyons of southern Utah and the Arizona strip to the Crossing of the Fathers.

Those who know history will object that Escalante wasn't alone. He wasn't even in charge. Father Francisco Atanasio Dominguez was the leader. There was also Don Bernardo Miera y Pacheco, the veteran soldier and engineer who drew that famous first map of the Utah country. There was Andres Muniz, the experienced and knowledgeable interpreter. Six other men shared the hardships, and the honor, of the journey.

But it was Escalante who, along with Father Francisco Garces, made the most untiring efforts to open a trail linking the missions in New Mexico to those in California. It was Escalante whose preliminary expedition discovered that the trail had to swing north through Utah. And, possibly most important of all to his place in history, it was Escalante who kept the record. Whatever contribution others made, in this account the expedition will carry Escalante's name.

So, what were a couple of New Mexico-based Catholic priests doing wandering around the Great Basin in the first place? The answer requires some historical background.

Nearly two centuries after the Spaniards in Old Mexico had pushed up the Rio Grande to establish an anchor at Santa Fe, they turned their attention to the tawny shores of California. Father Serra founded the Mission of San Diego in 1769, the first in California. By 1773, four other missions were struggling for survival. But they were starving. A way had to be found to supply them from the settlements prospering along the Rio Grande. Besides, if Spain could tie together these outposts of empire and settle some of the country between, she would control a vast and, as it turned out, wealthy region.

The effort was heroic. In 1775, Escalante set out from Zuni, New Mexico to explore a trail to California. He reached the Hopis, who, atop their rugged mesas, had long resisted Spanish authority. At Oraibi, then as now the oldest continuously inhabited village in North America, he found the Hopis hostile and unwilling to hear about Christianity. The same report came the following year from Father Garces, who had made a solitary horseback expedition from his base in Yuma into the San Joaquin Valley, then east to the Havasupai Indians in Grand Canyon, and finally to Oraibi. There the Hopis refused him even a place to sleep.

Things haven't changed that much. Some years ago, we drove through the Hopi mesas and turned off to Oraibi. Halfway down the dusty dirt road was a hand-lettered sign: *"White men, turn back. You don't respect our religion or our ways. You are not welcome."* Other Hopis waved us on, to where a Kachina Corn Dance was in progress, but we had learned what Escalante and Garces learned two centuries earlier: the Hopis care deeply about their ancient religion and don't welcome efforts to change it.

Between them, Escalante and Garces had found a way to California across the dry and deeply-scarred country of northern Arizona. But both agreed that because of the hostility of the Hopis and of the Apaches along the Gila River, a better way had to found.

The Escalante expedition of 1776 was charged to find that way. Earlier Spanish trading expeditions into Western Colorado had established a trail as far as the Gunnison River, and the Ute Indians in that region had proven friendly. Why not follow that known trail and then swing west into the unknown to see what could be found?

That was the decision. July 4, 1776 was the date to begin. But Escalante fell ill. This and other problems pushed back departure to July 29. As it turned out, that delay meant the expedition would never reach Monterey. It also meant that the party would neither follow their own tracks back to Santa Fe nor return, as intended, by way of the Havasupai villages south of the Grand Canyon. Instead, they would wander through, and nearly perish in, some of the harshest, most difficult terrain on earth, the Canyonlands of southern Utah.

But that was in the unknown future. With ebullient hopes and *"under the patronage of the Virgin Mary, Our Lady of the Immaculate Conception, and of the most holy patriarch Joseph her most happy spouse,"* the explorers struck north from Santa Fe. Father Dominguez, supervisor of the Franciscan missions in New Mexico, was in charge, but he was far less experienced in wilderness travel than Father Escalante. Don Miera, a veteran of thirty years on the New Mexico frontier, carried an astrolab, a quadrant, and a compass; he would chart the party's progress with astronomical observations and produce the first map of this region. From earlier trading expeditions, Andres Muniz knew the trail through western Colorado; more important, he knew the Ute language and would prove invaluable as interpreter. The expedition rode Spanish horses and drove a train of pack mules carrying provisions and equipment as well as gifts to woo the Indians they would

encounter. A herd of cattle would provide food.

Their route into and through western Colorado would logically have entered Utah south of the LaSal Mountains, as did the Spanish Trail half a century later. Indeed, they came within a few miles of the present border, from where Escalante named and described the LaSal and Abajo Mountains. But after wandering for three days trying to find a way out of the canyons of the Gunnison River, they faced a decision: should they push on west through the arid and formidable canyons of the Colorado Plateau, or work their way farther north to avoid the canyon country? One argument for going north was that this route would take them to Utah Lake, where, they had heard, lived a sedentary and peaceful tribe of Indians who might be ripe for conversion to Christianity.

"Everyone had a different opinion," Escalante recorded on August 20. *"So, finding ourselves in this state of confusion . . . we put our trust in God and our will in that of His Most Holy Majesty. And, having implored the intercession of our Most Holy Patrons in order that God might direct us in the way that would be most conducive to His Holy Service, we cast lots . . . "*

The northern route won. So, swinging first northeast and then northwest in a long arc, and picking up an Indian boy from the Utah Lake tribe to act as guide—they named him Silvestre— the explorers crossed the White River near Rangeley and entered Utah just east of present-day Jensen. The date was September 11.

Here in lush, grassy meadows under the

great Permian sandstone wall where the Green River carves its way through Split Mountain, Escalante and his party stopped to rest their hoof-sore horses. One day was spent killing a buffalo after a seven-mile chase on the expedition's swiftest horses. On another day, Joaquin, a second Indian boy from Utah Lake, *"as a prank mounted a very fiery horse. While galloping across the meadow, the horse caught his forefeet in a hole and fell, throwing the rider a long distance. We were frightened, thinking that the Laguna had been badly hurt by the fall because when he had recovered from his fright, he wept copious tears. But God was pleased that the only damage was that done to the horse which completely broke its neck, leaving it useless."*

The party spent five days in this pleasant spot under the twisted white-and-tan cliffs of Split Mountain. Escalante's is the first recorded description of that remarkable gash in the mountains through which so many modern rapids-loving river runners have whooped their way. The river, he wrote, flows *"between two high cliffs which, after forming a sort of corral, come so close together that one can scarcely see the opening through which the river comes."*

On September 16, the explorers forded the Green River, which they had been told was the boundary between the Ute and Comanche nations. Today, a monument at the entrance to Dinosaur National Monument marks the crossing. Silvestre then led the ten explorers downstream along the north bank of the Green River, crossing Brush and Ashley Creeks, to the Horseshoe Bend of the

Lichen-encrusted boulder in Uinta mountain meadow. Escalante passed just south of here in 1776.
George Wuerthner

Green, then west across dry, gravelly benchlands to the Duchesne River at present-day Randlett.

To pick up the trail, the modern explorer heads south from Highway 40, fifteen miles from Vernal, on State Highway 88. This is lovely country. The fat pheasant cocks we saw along the highway on a crisp September morning would have been unknown to Escalante. But not the herd of antelope that browsed along the road and disappeared in a flash of white rumps before a camera could focus. And certainly not the vast and diverse flocks of waterfowl on Pelican Lake and along the Duchesne.

From Randlett, the highway-shunner can follow a dirt road that parallels the south side of the Duchesne River. This is Indian reservation, with a television dish squatting in front of every mobile home. Fat black cows graze on alfalfa stubble. Indians drive four-wheel-drive pickups across the fields to tend their sprinklers. Huge cottonwood trees in golden leaf line the river as it snakes through the meadows. Abandoned houses dot the fields, paneless windows staring like empty eye sockets.

At Myton, the river, and the trail, cross north of Highway 40, and again there are back-country roads to follow in order to appreciate Escalante's exasperation with the tough going. *"Because the guide wanted to cross over to the river's other side and follow it,"* he wrote, *"he stuck us through an almost impenetrable osier bosque, or thicket, and into marshy estuaries which made us backtrack and cross the river thrice while making many useless detours."* The willow thickets and marshes are still there.

Still ascending the river, the party reached the present site of Duchesne on September 18. A monument now marks the campsite. Here, Miera calculated, they were 287 leagues—over 750 miles—from Santa Fe, which they had left fifty-one days earlier.

Despite the willows, Escalante liked this country. He wrote: *"There is good land along these three rivers we crossed today, and plenty of it for farming with the aid of irrigation—beautiful poplar groves, fine pastures, timber and firewood not too far away, for three good settlements."* Early settlers who struggled to survive early frost and long drought here 150 years later thought less of the land. My grandfather, a Uintah Basin pioneer, used to chuckle over the story of the homesteader who sold a quarter section to an unsuspecting outsider.

"How much land did you sell him?" a neighbor asked. *"He bought 160 acres. But,"* in a behind-the-hand whisper, *"I slipped in an extra ten."*

Chances are an oil well now pumps away—or stands idle—on that extra ten. The oil boom of the 1970s brought unprecedented prosperity to the Uintah Basin until the glut of the 1980s restored the customary hard times.

Escalante foresaw none of that. Pushing on hard, he and his companions left the Duchesne River and headed west roughly along the present-day route of Highway 40. *"At the plain's end we descended by a high ridge, rocky and steep, to the water source, which we named San Eustaquio,"* Escalante wrote, describing what is now known as Red

Creek, where there was then and still is *"abundant pasturage."* This was a long march, twenty-five miles. *"We arrived very tired, both on account of the day's march's painful travel and because a very cold west wind did not cease blowing very hard all day long,"* he wrote. The date was September 19, and a September day in that country may still not be so different.

Another long day, 23.5 miles took them up Deep Creek nearly to the summit now overlooking Strawberry Reservoir. *"Tonight it was so cold that even the water which stood close to the fire all night was frozen by morning,"* Escalante complained. Tough going for padres used to New Mexico's gentle winters. But there was much worse to come.

From the summit, Highway 40 closely follows the trail to the edge of Strawberry Reservoir. The explorers descended Strawberry River, describing *"a very pleasant valley with good pasturages, many springs, and beautiful groves of not very tall or thick white poplars* [aspen]. *In it are all the conveniences required for a settlement."* The valley is now under water.

From here, the explorers struck west to climb over the Wasatch. With no trail, and annoyed by guides who frequently hurried on out of sight, they struggled through what Escalante described as *"a dense forest of white poplar, scruboak, chokecherry, and spruce . . . which became denser the more we advanced, and after going west for half a league* [a little more than a mile] *we emerged from it, arriving at a very lofty ridge."*

Here, at the 8200-foot summit, Escalante left the Colorado River drainage and got his first view of the Great Basin. To weary travelers, the view must have been daunting. Spread before them lay a great drainage system—First Water, Fifth Water, Sixth Water, Shingle, and Mill Fork creeks, fanning off from the ridge like the fingers of a hand, all draining into Diamond Fork and eventually into Spanish Fork and Utah Lake.

Escalante wrote: *"The guide pointed out to us the side on which the lake lay, and to the southeast of it the other side of the sierra where he told us there lived a greater number of people of the same language and type as the Lagunas."* So the expedition's first major goal was in sight. But between it and where they stood lay a wilderness of densely forested slopes plunging into deep canyons, with no discernible way through.

A jeep road now ascends the ridge from Strawberry. At the summit, a sign warns: *"Hazardous road ahead . . . Four-wheel drive recommended . . . Impassable in wet weather."* After negotiating the mammoth ruts and steep switchbacks, we were believers.

For Escalante, there was no road, not even a trail. He was here on September 22, 1776. The maple, oak, and aspen must have been in glorious color, but his marvelously detailed and descriptive journal makes no mention of that. The frustration and difficulty of fighting a way down those trackless slopes make the omission understandable. The journal is painfully explicit:

"Along this ridge we went southwest for a quarter league and descended it, break-

ing through almost impenetrable swaths of chokecherry and scruboak and passing through another poplar forest so thick that we doubted if the packs could get through unless they were first taken off. In this forest the guide again began annoying us with his haste, so that we had to hold him back and never leave him to himself. In this dense growth Padre Fray Francisco Atanasio got a hard blow on one knee against a poplar tree."

After a long day, they "descended with great difficulty and labor into a deep and narrow valley [Sixth Water Creek] and camped." The next day, as they were still in this ridge-and-canyon wilderness, was no better: "On the 22nd we set out . . . along this narrow valley's north slope, on which there were many dangerous defiles and slides, with no other trail than the one we went opening all along, and over the sierra's corrugated ruggedness which all over here made us change direction and wind about excessively at every step . . ." They finally camped near the present Palmyra campground on Diamond Fork.

Smoke on nearby ridges signaled that the Laguna Indians they had come so far to see were aware of their presence. "We returned the message," Escalante wrote, "to avoid being mistaken, should they have seen us, for hostile people and so have them run away or welcome us with arrows. Again they began sending up bigger smoke clouds at the pass through which we had to go toward the lake—and this made us believe that they had already seen us, for this is the handiest and the regular signal used for anything worth

knowing about all the peoples in this part of America."

On September 23, Escalante entered Utah Valley, descending Diamond Fork to Spanish Fork River, down past the meadows now buried by the Thistle landslide, through the narrows of lower Spanish Fork Canyon, and out onto the old Lake Bonneville bench, where they "caught sight of the lake and spreading valley of Nuestra Senora de la Merced of the Timpanogotzis"—a more charming name, certainly, than the present one. Surrounded by smoke signals as well as smoke from meadows that the fearful Indians had set afire, Escalante made camp on the Spanish Fork River, just about at the junction of I-15 and Highway 6.

But for four of the party, it was not time to rest. To allay the Indians' fears, Father Atanasio, sore knee and all, rode ahead with the two Lagunas, Silvestre and Joaquin, and Muniz the interpreter, "racing the horses . . . to the point of exhaustion" to reach the Laguna camp on Utah Lake at the mouth of Provo River. Escalante describes their reception:

"Some men came out to meet them with weapons in hand to defend their homes and families, but as soon as Silvestre spoke to them the show of war was changed into the finest and fondest expressions of peace and affection. They very joyfully conducted them to their little humble abodes, and after he had embraced each single one and let them know that we came in peace, and that we loved them as our greatest friends, the padre allowed them time to talk at length with our guide Silvestre, who gave them an account

so much in our favor of what he had observed and witnessed ever since he had become one of us, and about our purpose in coming, that we could not have wished for a better report."

Runners sped to outlying villages, spreading word of the strange visitors. With the tribe assembled, the teaching began. The padres explained "the motives for our coming, and that the principal one was to seek the salvation of their souls and to show them the only means whereby they could attain it—the chief, primary, and necessary one being to believe in a single true God, to love Him and obey Him wholly by doing what is contained in His holy and spotless Law— and that all this would be taught them with greater clarity and at greater length, and the water of holy baptism poured on them . . ."

Then came the clincher: "Should they wish to become Christians," the padres promised, others would "come to instruct them and Spaniards to live among them, and that in this event they would be taught how to farm and to raise livestock, whereby they would then have everything necessary in food and clothing, just like the Spaniards. For, by submitting themselves to live in the manner ordered by God and as the padres would teach them, our Great Chief whom we call King would send them everything that was needed . . ."

Ignorant of the semi-slavery that had followed such promises made to Indians in New Mexico and elsewhere, the Lagunas agreed. They "offered all their land to the Spaniards for them to build their homes wherever they pleased" and promised to guard against the

dreaded Comanches. They willingly sold dried fish to replenish the expedition's dwindling supplies and provided a guide to the country south and west.

The hour for departure arrived on September 25, and Escalante wrote: *"All bade us farewell most tenderly, especially Silvestre, who hugged us tightly, practically in tears. And they began charging us once more not to delay our return too long, saying that they expected us back within a year."*

That Escalante hoped and expected to return, there seems little doubt. His journal included a glowing report of Utah Valley, describing the four rivers that irrigate it—American Fork, Provo, Hobble Creek, Spanish Fork—the excellent soil, the timber in the mountains, and the abundant waterfowl and fish in and around the lake. *"And,"* he added, *"the climate here is a good one, for, after having experienced cold aplenty since we left El Rio de San Buenaventura [the Green River], we felt warm throughout the entire valley by day and by night."* Miera added his testimony: *"the most pleasing, beautiful and fertile site in all New Spain."*

Finally, Escalante described the Indians themselves, who were, after all, the most important resource favoring Spanish settlement: *"Their dwellings are some sheds or little wattle huts of osier [willows], out of which they have interestingly crafted baskets and other instruments of ordinary use. They are very poor as regards dress. The most becoming one they wear is a deerskin jacket and long leggings of the same. For cold seasons*

they wear blankets made of jackrabbit and coney rabbit furs. They employ the Yuta language but with noticeable variances in pronunciation, and even in some words. They possess good features, and most of them are fully bearded. All the sections of this sierra along the southeast, south-southwest, and west are inhabited by a great number of peoples of the same nation, language, and easy-going character as these Lagunas, with whom a very populous and extensive province could be formed."

As for the *"other lake"* they heard about to the north [Great Salt Lake], *"its waters are harmful and extremely salty, for the Timpanois assured us that anyone who wet some part of the body with them immediately felt a lot of itching in the part moistened."* Besides, the Lagunas warned, *"all around it lives a numerous and secluded nation calling itself Puaguampe, which in our common speech means 'bewitched'."*

In summary, Escalante reported, the valley of Nuestra Senora de la Merced of the Timpanogotzis so invited settlement that *"if each town took only one league of farmland, as many Indian pueblos can fit inside the valley as there are those in New Mexico."* Surely, his superiors in New Mexico could not reject his recommendation to return, Christianize the Indians, and settle there.

As it turned out, they did. The Indians did not see another white man until Spanish traders reached Utah Valley thirty years later. It would be twenty more years before the first American trappers arrived. As for white

men coming to settle among and Christianize them, that would wait three-quarters of a century for the Mormons. One of the most intriguing *"what ifs"* of history is what if the padres had returned? What if the Spaniards had colonized this valley and other valleys Escalante was soon to see to the south? Would Utah's culture today be New Mexico-style Spanish instead of Anglo-Saxon Mormon?

But Monterey awaited, and the season was late. The expedition now hurried south, generally following the present-day route of I-15; modern highway builders and Spanish explorers both looked for the best combination of straight-line distance and easy terrain. It is also no coincidence that their campsites were at or near places now known as Springville, Spanish Fork, Payson, Mona, Levan, Yuba, and Scipio. Both town builders and trailfinders like grass and water.

From Yuba, the explorers could have followed the Sevier River west to Sevier Lake before pushing on west through Nevada to California. Instead, they continued south, through Scipio Pass, then west into the Black Rock desert. It was tough going, with alkali flats and mirages and no water fit to drink after thirty-six thirsty miles of travel. From a dry camp five miles northwest of volcanic Pavant Butte, the horse herd was driven ahead by moonlight toward a reported waterhole. They didn't find it, the herd wandered off, and daybreak of October 2 found the party in serious straits.

Indians saved them. From their village on

the banks of the Sevier River came a band of Indians with beards so long they reminded Escalante of Capuchin priests. As they had at Utah Lake, the padres preached the Gospel to these Indians and promised that they and other Spaniards would return, baptize and live among them.

"They all replied very joyfully that we must come back with the other padres," Escalante wrote, *"that they would do what-soever we taught them and ordered them to do . . . We took our leave of them, and all, the chief especially, kept holding us by the hand with great tenderness and affec-tion . . . Scarcely did they see us depart when all—following their chief, who started first—burst out crying copious tears, so that even when we were quite a distance away we kept hearing the tender laments of these unfortunate little sheep of Christ, lost along the way simply for not having the Light. They touched our hearts so much that some of our companions could not hold back the tears."*

Thirty-seven years later, these *"unfor-tunate little sheep,"* perhaps disillusioned and embittered by their fruitless wait for the padres' return, sent the Arze-Garcia trading expedition fleeing for their lives. Forty years after that, in 1853, descendants of these same little sheep expressed their feelings not by weeping tender tears but by slaughtering Captain J. W. Gunnison and six of his men.

From their meeting with the bearded Utes, the Escalante expedition pushed on south into the area of Clear Lake. The marshes there that today teem with waterfowl on a wild-

life refuge gave the 1776 travelers only a hard time. After several detours around the marshes, they decided to cross one. *"The ford was sticky and miry,"* Escalante reported, *"and in it the mount which Andres the interpreter was riding fell and pitched him into the water, dealing him a hard blow on the cheek."*

Finally, escaping the marshes, they reached the arroyo of the Beaver River, mostly dry at this season. Following it, and generally paralleling the present-day Union Pacific railroad tracks and Highway 257, they crossed a low pass into the northern end of what later was named the Escalante Desert. Here, trouble came in bunches, and it was here that the exploration to California was aborted.

First, two members of the expedition, probably frustrated by the hard going, fell into an argument that degenerated into a fist fight. Frightened by such unaccustomed vio-lence, the Laguna who had guided them south from Utah Lake *"turned back and left us without an adieu . . . We tried to con-vince him that those involved were not angry with each other, and that even when a par-ent corrected his youngster as it now had happened, they never reached the point of killing each other as he was thinking, and therefore that he should not be scared. Nevertheless, he turned back from here, while we were left without anyone who knew about the country ahead, even if from hearsay."*

Next, two men sent to explore a way west

over the Beaver Mountains returned after dark with a discouraging report, *"saying that they had not found any pass for traversing the sierra, that it was very high and rugged from this direction, and that ahead of it lay a wide plain without any pasturage or water source whatsoever. This being so, we could no longer take this direction—which was best for getting to Monterey, where our goal lay—and we decided to continue south . . . "*

Then came the real trouble. *"On the preceding days a very cold wind from the south had blown fiercely without ceasing. This brought on a snowfall so heavy that not only the sierra's heights but even all the plains were covered with snow tonight."* Snow continued throughout the next day, October 6, stopping only after *"we implored the intercession of Our Mother and Patro-ness by praying aloud in common the three parts of her rosary and by chanting the Litany, the one of All-Saints."*

Next day, Escalante made only this bleak entry: *"On the 7th we could not depart . . . either, although we were in great distress, without firewood and extremely cold, for with so much snow and water the ground, which was soft here, was unfit for travel."*

This snowbound camp was on the deso-late flats a couple of miles west of Black Rock. A place more likely to take the heart out of a man is hard to imagine. The next day was no better. Only those who know the slick and sticky gumbo of the Escalante Desert after a storm can begin to appreciate the misery reflected by Escalante's entry on

Left: Sunrise over the Wah Wah Valley. The grim, waterless prospects of such country in the Escalante desert turned the expe-dition back from its California goal.
John George

Right: Paria River Canyon. The Escalante expedition scaled the walls of this canyon to escape the Colorado River camp it called Salsipuedes—"Get out if you can."
Stephen Trimble

The waters of Lake Powell at Padre Bay inundated the Crossing of the Fathers where, on November 7, 1776, the Escalante expedition finally found its way down to and across the Colorado River.
Frank Jensen

October 8: *"We travel only three leagues and a half* [nine miles] *with great difficulty, because it was so soft and miry everywhere that many pack animals and mounts, and even those that were loose, either fell down or became stuck altogether . . . we suffered greatly from the cold because the north wind did not cease blowing all day, and most acutely."*

It was more than enough, even for men of such commitment and fortitude. On that miserable day, October 8, Monterey was forsaken.

Escalante was at pains to detail the reasons for the unhappy decision. First, after traveling seventy-seven days, they advanced only some 350 miles west and, Escalante lamented, had *"many leagues"*—actually more than 500 miles—yet to go. Second, winter had come, the mountains were snowed in, provisions were low, and *"we could expose ourselves to perishing from hunger if not from the cold."* Third, even if they could reach Monterey, they couldn't get back to Santa Fe before the next June, which would mean a long delay in returning to the Lagunas and the bearded Indians. Escalante feared they *"would feel frustrated in their hopes, or they would conclude that we had purposely deceived them. As a result, their conversion and the extension of his majesty's dominions in this direction would become much more difficult in the future."* Finally, by heading south the expedition might discover a shorter and better route back to Santa Fe.

So they headed south, but some were not pleased with the decision. Miera, the mapmaker-engineer, was particularly disgrun-

tled because, Escalante wrote, he had conceived *"grandiose dreams of honors and profit from solely reaching Monterey and had imparted them to the rest by building castles in the air of the loftiest."*

After traveling two days with bickering that Escalante called *"extremely onerous, and all unbearably irksome,"* they determined for the second time to seek direction from a higher source. *"And so, in order that God's cause stood better justified, and to make them understand more clearly that we had changed our mind neither out of fear nor by our own despotic will, we decided to lay aside altogether the great weight of the arguments mentioned and, after imploring the divine mercy and the intercession of our holy patron saints, to search anew God's will by casting lots—putting Monterey on one and Cosnina on the other—and to follow the route which came out."*

Cosnina—that is, the Havasupais on the south side of Grand Canyon—came out. It is a testament to the faithfulness of these travel-weary men that the bickering ended.

This casting of lots took place October 11 on the barren flats of the Escalante Desert, just south of Blue Knoll and halfway between Milford and Cedar City. The decision made, the ten men now moved rapidly south, through Horse Hollow into Cedar Valley, passing the Three Peaks and Quichapa Lake west of Cedar City, and reaching Kanarra Creek just west of present-day Kanarraville. They descended the creek to its junction with Ash Creek, which they followed into Ash Creek Canyon, described by Escalante as *"a ridge cut entirely of black lava rock which lies between two high sierras."* Every traveler on this section where I-15 rims out of the Great Basin and plunges down over Black Ridge has seen the place.

Here, a fearful Indian the expedition had bribed near Cedar City slipped away and fled. *"Bereft of a guide, we continued south for a league with great hardship on account of so much rock."* Escalante wasn't alone in complaining about this passage beneath the towering Hurricane Cliffs. One of the Mormon pioneers sent three-quarters of a century later to colonize Dixie recalled: *"There's only one bump on that road—but it's forty miles long."*

As they had with Indians to the north, the padres tried hard to convince the Indians they encountered here that they were loved as brothers. But privately, Escalante had little good to say about the Shivwit and other Paiute tribes of southern Utah. He found them timorous and deceitful, nearly naked, and living in wretched conditions. Some women gathering seeds in Cedar Valley, he wrote, *"were so poorly dressed that they wore only some pieces of deerskin hanging from the waist, barely covering what one cannot gaze upon without peril."*

In general, he wrote, these Indians *"are extremely low-spirited and different from the Lagunas and from the* [full-bearded] *Barbones."* The difference would be cruelly demonstrated during the next half-century as the Utes to the north made a profitable business of capturing and selling as slaves their southern Utah cousins.

On October 13, the padres camped at present Toquerville and wrote the first description of the mild, warm climate of Utah's Dixie. They would be far from the last to drop over Black Ridge to escape the wintry bitterness of the Great Basin high country. The welcome warmth continued the next day as they pushed on south for 26.5 miles, passing LaVerkin Creek and the sulphurous Virgin River and continuing below the Hurricane Cliffs to camp just below what would be the Arizona line.

Here, their food gave out, and Indians warned they could not continue south to the Colorado *"because there were no water sources, nor could we cross the river by this route for its being very much boxed in and very deep, and having extremely tall rocks and cliffs along both sides"*—a fair description of the Grand Canyon. Instead, the Indians reported, there was a ford over the Colorado directly to the east.

The padres mistrusted and ignored this advice—a decision they would bitterly regret. Desperately hungry, they pushed southeast deeper into northern Arizona to get around the Hurricane Cliffs, then turned northeast up Kimball Valley to re-enter Utah briefly west of the Paria River. Turning south again to avoid the Paria Plateau, then northeast to the rim of Marble Canyon, they finally reached the Colorado River at what became Lees Ferry on October 26.

This ten-day struggle through northern Arizona had been a frightful ordeal. Without a guide, able to buy only tiny amounts of food from timid Indians who were themselves hungry, they had rimrocked themselves on trackless mesas, backtracked around awesome gorges, became ill, suffered cruelly from thirst and hunger. Twice they had been forced to kill horses for food.

But what lay ahead was worse. This spot where the Paria River enters the Colorado, the present-day launching site for float trips through Grand Canyon, is the one place for fifty miles upstream and 150 miles down that a horse could reasonably reach the river. A century later, John D. Lee would build a ferry here and carve the roughest kind of road up the cliffs on the opposite side. But there was no ferry in 1776. And the river was wide and deep.

"This afternoon [the day of arrival] *we decided to find out if after crossing the river we could continue from here toward the southeast or east,"* Escalante wrote. To do the exploring, *"two of those who knew how to swim well entered the river naked with their clothes upon their heads. It was so deep and wide that the swimmers, in spite of their prowess, were barely able to reach the other side, leaving in midstream their clothing, which they never saw again. And since they became so exhausted getting there, nude and barefoot, they were unable to walk far enough to do the said exploring, coming back across after having paused a while to catch their breath."* Clearly, this was not the ford the Indians had told them about.

With that bleak result, knowing how difficult the backtrack would be, and *"surrounded on all sides by mesas and big hogbacks impossible to climb"* [Vermillion and Echo Cliffs], it's understandable that the discouraged padres named this camp Salsipuedes—*"get out if you can".*

They almost didn't. Don Juan Pedro Cis-

Sunrise over Navajo Mountain.
The Crossing of the Fathers is a few
miles downstream from this point.
John George

neros explored up Paria Creek to find a way up to the mesa above. Today's hikers in that magnificent vertical-walled canyon will understand how he could travel a day and part of a night and find no way. Others explored upriver and *"found nothing but insuperable obstacles for getting to the ford without retracing much terrain."* They tried a raft, but even with fifteen-foot poles could not reach the bottom of this powerful river. Finally, the Muniz brothers were sent back up the Paria with orders to keep going until they found a way out, and then to follow the rim above the Colorado until they found the ford.

A day of anxious waiting, and another horse was slaughtered. Another day. And another. On the fourth day, November 1, the brothers returned, reporting they had found a *"high and steeply rugged"* ascent out of the Paria and had then found the ford. Camp was quickly moved 2.6 miles up the Paria to the foot of the ascent. The climb next day was three hours of terror, up what Escalante called *"extremely difficult stretches and most dangerous ledges, and at the very last impassable."* But they passed it, reaching the top 1700 feet above the Colorado, and camped above the present-day swimming beach at Wahweap.

Two more days of struggling across the mesas, and on November 3 they again reached the rim above the river, opposite the mouth of Navajo Canyon. They had learned that in this country getting in does not necessarily mean getting out. They also learned, to their disgust, that the Muniz brothers had found no ford—had not, in fact, even

reached this place. So they sent Juan Domingo and Lucrecio Muniz to swim the river a second time and explore for a possible exit.

"The descent to the river is very long, steep, rugged, and precipitous," Escalante wrote, *"consisting of such terrible rock embankments that two pack animals which descended the first one could not make it back, even without the equipment."*

The only meal the next day, while waiting the scouts' return, was roasted prickly pear cactus and some tiny berries from the river. And again, disappointment; Domingo reported there was no way out. Muniz was still missing, but they could wait no longer on this waterless, foodless mesa. They pushed on northeast, making only 7.5 miles *"over many ridges and gullies."* To add to their misery, *"Tonight it rained heavily here, and it snowed in some places. It was raining at daybreak and kept it up for some hours."*

Still no sign of Lucrecio Muniz, which *"caused us plenty of worry, because he had been three days without provisions and no covering, other than his shirt, since he had not even taken trousers along."* With meat from the most recently slaughtered horse, Lucrecio's brother was sent in search. By nightfall of the next day he showed up with his hardy but not very reliable brother in tow.

November 6 was another day of misery. *"After we had gone three leagues* [almost seven miles] *we were stopped for a long time by a strong blizzard and tempest consisting of rain and thick hailstones amid horren-*

dous thunder claps and lightning flashes. We recited the Virgin's Litany, for her to implore some relief for us, and God willed for the tempest to end."

The storm's end was a good omen. Another mile of travel and they stopped for what would be their last camp west of the river. Cisneros came back to report he had reached the rim above the Colorado, that the river was very wide and apparently not deep, that there was a way—a very difficult way—down a nearby side canyon. They had found, at last, the Ute crossing.

This last campsite is now deep under the waters of Lake Powell, as is most of the route the explorers had followed from the Paria. So, of course, is the final descent to the Crossing of the Fathers.

The descent down Padre Creek on November 7 proved easier than much of what they had already done. Of it, Escalante wrote simply: *"We went out very early to inspect the canyon and ford, taking along the two mixed-breeds, Felipe and Juan Domingo, so that they might ford the river on foot since they were good swimmers. In order to have the mounts led down to the canyon mentioned, it became necessary to cut steps with axes on a stone cliff for the space of three yards or a bit less. Over the rest of it the horse herds were able to get across, although without pack or rider."* Later explorers found those steps in 1937 and placed a bronze plaque at the site.

But now came the crucial test: Could the river be crossed? After descending to the river, Escalante wrote, they *"went along it downstream about two musket shots some-*

times in the water, sometimes on the bank, until we reached the widest part of its current where the ford appeared to be. One of the men waded in and found it good, not having to swim at any place. We followed him on horseback, entering a little farther down, and in its middle two mounts which went ahead missed bottom and swam through a short channel. We held back, although with some peril, until the first one who crossed on foot came back from the other side to lead us, and we successfully passed over without the horses on which we were crossing ever having to swim.''

It was the padres' good fortune that their crossing was in the fall, when the river was at its lowest. Attempting a crossing in spring or until late summer would have been disastrous.

The rest was anticlimax. Signals were given to the men above, who lowered packs and saddles down the vertical cliff with ropes and lassos. The horse herd was driven down and across. By 5 p.m. it was finished, with the entire party *"praising God our Lord and firing off some muskets in demonstration of the great joy we all felt in having overcome so great a problem."*

Safely on the homeward side, Escalante found time for reflection. With a guide to point out the water holes, and heading east from the Virgin along the present-day Arizona-Utah state line, they could have reached the Crossing in five or six days instead of three-and-a-half weeks of perilous suffering. But, the faith-filled Escalante philosophized, *"God doubtless disposed that we obtained no guide, either as merciful*

chastisement for our faults or so that we could acquire some knowledge of the peoples living hereabouts."

Escalante also took time here to describe the Colorado Plateau country generally and the five tribes of Ute-speaking Indians found there. But he made no recommendation that this was any place for Spanish proselyting or settlements.

Following trails made by Indians and wild sheep, the explorers found their way out of the gorge and to the top of Weed Bench, where they lost the trail and found themselves rimrocked and suffering from bitter cold. They spent two days wandering on the mesa and trying to persuade a few timid Indians to show them the way. Eventually, they found the lost trail and followed it into and out of Navajo Canyon, *"making many turns and passing some rock shelves which are perilous and improvable only by dint of crowbars."* The trail *"has some dangerous stretches and all of it is precipitous,"* Escalante reported, but *"the Indians have fixed it up with loose stones and sticks, and in the last one they have a stairway of the same, more than three yards long and two wide."* Evidence of that work can still be seen.

Navajo Canyon was the last major obstacle. Rimming out and now traveling in open—but bitter cold—country, the party hastened south and east, reaching the ancient Hopi settlement of Oraibi on November 16. Here at last they were able to buy food enough to push on to the pueblo and mission of Zuni, arriving there on November 24. Exhausted, they rested until December 13,

then traveled on to Santa Fe, their starting place. On January 2, 1777, 184 days after their adventure began, they reached home.

Epilogue. On Dominguez' return to Santa Fe, he found he had been relieved as head of the New Mexico missions; he had been, apparently, too blunt and strict for some of his colleagues. He died in obscurity as chaplain of the Presidio of Janos in Sonora at the age of sixty-five.

Escalante's career prospered even less. He spent a year as missionary friar to the Indian pueblo of San Ildefonso in 1777, but a kidney ailment forced him to Mexico City for treatment. He died there in 1780.

So they failed. The trail linking Santa Fe and Los Angeles would be made by others. Except for a section already known through northern New Mexico and southwestern Colorado, it would follow little of their route, owe little to their efforts. The Catholic fathers in Mexico rejected their appeals to colonize, and there would be no Spanish missionaries to Utah Lake Indians. They left no trace on the land, and it is difficult to see where their trek benefited any future trailmakers.

But if daring and resourcefulness, intelligence and perseverance have value, their journey was not a failure. They accomplished what from this time and distance seems impossible. They saw land and people no white man had ever seen, and Escalante understood and described them as few others ever would. They traveled 2,000 miles through some of the most inhospitable land on the continent, lost none of their party along the way, and left nothing but friends behind. History knows few if any greater successes.

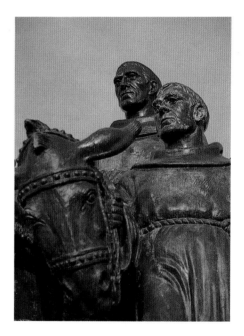

Dominguez and Escalante statue, This Is the Place Monument, Salt Lake City
Rick Reese

Boulder field, Stansbury Island. Jedediah Smith called the Great Salt Lake his "home in the wilderness."

John George

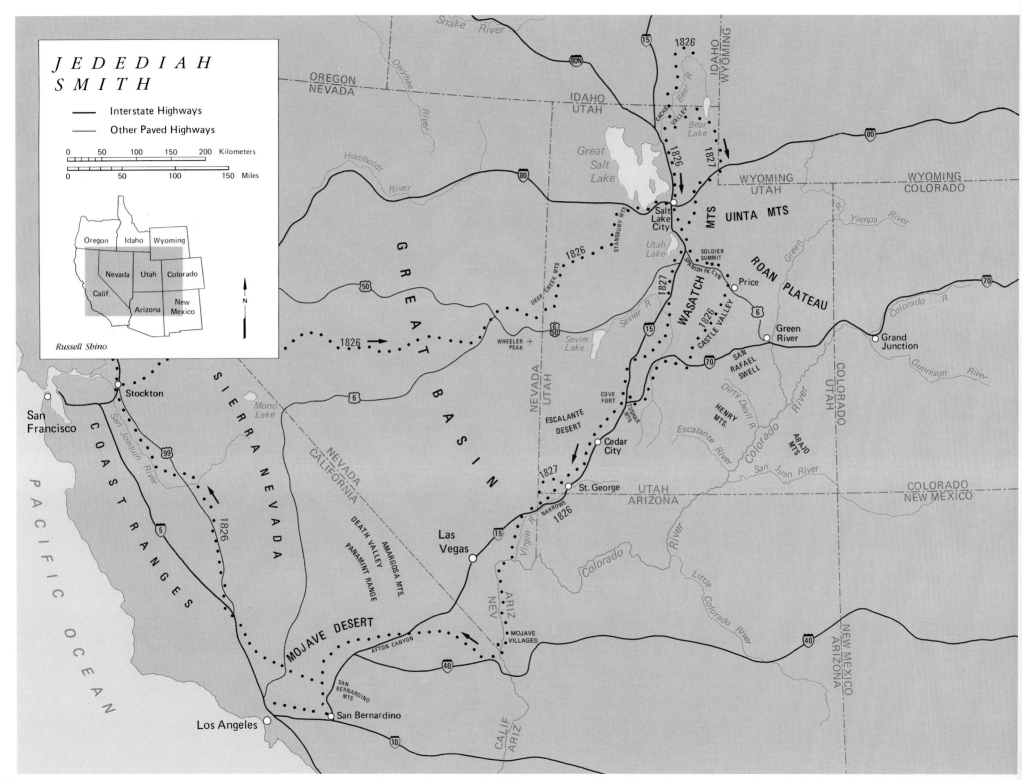

JEDEDIAH
SMITH

⸺ Interstate Highways
⸺ Other Paved Highways

0   50   100   150   200 Kilometers
0   50   100   150 Miles

Russell Shino

Oregon Idaho Wyoming
Nevada Utah Colorado
Calif. Arizona New Mexico

N

JEDEDIAH SMITH

If one name stands above all others in the making of Utah trails, it is that of Jedediah Strong Smith. In fact, with the debatable exception of Meriwether Lewis and William Clark, no one left the first Anglo footprints on more miles of western wilderness.

This soft-spoken, Bible-carrying trailblazer came to the mountains in 1822 at age twenty-three. He left them eight years later. Within another year, he was dead, killed by Comanche lances on a lonely stretch of the Santa Fe trail.

During those eight years, Smith accomplished an astonishing number of firsts. He was first to open South Pass as the great route of western emigration; first to travel the north-to-south length of Utah; first to reach California from American soil, linking the trails blazed by Escalante and Garces fifty years earlier; first to cross the Sierra; first to cross the Great Basin, proving that no Buenaventura River flowed from Great Salt Lake to the Pacific Ocean; first to traverse the California and Oregon coasts to the Columbia. No man cut a wider and longer swath in the West. No man knew or understood it better.

And he was so different. His was the golden age of the Mountain Man, whose cussing, boozing, and whoring with Indian squaws were legendary. Into that milieu strode Jedediah—quiet, moral, deeply religious. He used no tobacco, did not drink, never swore. Apparently women did not tempt him—even in such places as the California missions where, one of his party wrote, the women *"thought it an honnour to ask a white man to sleep with them."*

Among men who competed to tell the most outrageous lies, he wrote journals that are not only literate but restrained and accurate.

If he had a flaw, it may have been a recklessness with his life and the lives of others. Perhaps his deep religious faith gave him a fatalism that led him into more than his share of troubles. He survived three Indian massacres that together killed thirty-nine of his companions. The first, by the Arikaris on the Missouri, was no fault of Smith's; he was a green recruit on the way to the Rockies with the William Ashley company. The second, by the Mojaves on the Colorado during his second journey to California, may be excused on the grounds that Smith could not have known the Mojaves were spoiling for revenge after a party of trappers under Ewing Young had killed some of the tribe. Still, Smith showed considerable incaution in leaving his party so vulnerable as they crossed the Colorado. As for the third attack, on the Umpqua River in Southern Oregon, anyone could have seen it coming as the Indians grew increasingly hostile. Smith later said that as he and two others left camp to scout out the country ahead he warned against letting the Indians into camp. But he was the leader, and responsibility was his.

His own death was characteristic of his bravery, his concern for others—and his recklessness. He was seeking a waterhole for his thirsty trading party along the inconstant Cimmaron River when the Comanches caught him. That's a noble effort, something he had done countless times. But sooner or later, disaster will overtake a man incautious enough to wander alone through country

infested with the most dangerous of all the plains Indians.

All this could hardly have been imagined by the tall young man who presented himself in 1822 in response to William Ashley's famous ad in the St. Louis Gazette for 100 *"Enterprising Young Men . . . to ascend the River Missouri to its source, there to be employed for one, two or three years . . ."* How he talked himself into a job as a hunter is hard to know; born and mostly raised in the east, he knew nothing about the frontier.

But he would learn—and fast. After wintering at the confluence of the Yellowstone and Missouri rivers, he was caught up in the Arikara massacre, where he showed such courage and leadership that Ashley named him captain of an independent party of trappers. He led them through the Dakota badlands and Black Hills onto the high plains of Wyoming, where a dramatic encounter with a grizzly bear cemented his reputation. James Clyman, also a greenhorn who would become one of the most famous Mountain Men, wrote an account that shows much of Jedediah's character:

" . . . while passing through a Brushy bottom a large Grissly came down the vally we being in single file men on foot leding pack horses he struck us about the center then turning ran paralel to our line Capt. Smith being in the advanc he ran to the open ground and as he emerged from the thicket he and the bear met face to face. Grissly did not hesitate a moment but sprung on the capt taking him by the head first pitcing sprawling on the earth he gave him a grab by the middle fortunately cathing by the ball

Jedediah Smith statue, This Is The Place Monument, Salt Lake City
Rick Reese

pouch and Butcher Kife which he broke but breaking several of his ribs and cutting his head badly."

Even with their leader in this condition, the trappers turned to him for decisions and instruction. Clyman continued:

"*. . . I asked the Capt what was best he said one or 2* [go] *for water and if you have a needle and thread git it out and sew up my wounds around my head which was bleeding freely I got a pair of scissors and cut off his hair and then began my first job of dessing wounds upon examination I* [found] *the bear had taken nearly all his head in his capcious mouth close to his left eye on one side and clos to his right ear on the other and laid the skull bare to near the crown of the head leaving a white streak whare his teeth passed one of his ears was torn from his head out to the outer rim after stitching all the other wounds in the best way I was capabl and according to the captains direction the ear being the last I told him I could do nothing for his Eare O you must try to stitch up some way or other said he then I put in my needle stiching it through and through and over and over laying the lacerated parts togather as nice as I could with my hands water was found in about ame* [one?] *mile when we all moved down and encamped the captain being able to mount his horse and to ride to camp whare we pitched a tent the onley one we had and made him as comfortable as the circumstances would permit this gave us lison on the charter of the grissly Baare which we did not forget . . .*"

Soon recovered but with scars he would carry the rest of his short life, Jedediah and his men wintered with Crow Indians on the Wind River. On a bitter cold day in March 1824, bracing against icy gales sweeping out of the north, he crossed South Pass. That historic day that opened the way for a vast tide of emigration was noted in Smith's journal mainly because his famished men killed a buffalo and devoured its meat raw as fast as they could cut it from the carcass.

Smith's wandering and trapping that year led him as far south as Black's Fork at the base of the Uinta Mountains, as far north as Clark's Fork on the Columbia River, and finally into winter camp on the Snake River with Peter Skene Ogden of the Hudson's Bay Company. The following July 1825, he met General Ashley, who had come out from St. Louis with a cargo of trade goods. Before the meeting, Ashley, in two boats made of buffalo hides, had made his remarkable descent of the Green through Flaming Gorge and on to the Uintah Basin.

Ashley and his capable young captain met on Henry's Fork of the Green River, just north of the Uintas. There, Ashley held the first of what would become the annual rendezvous for traders, trappers, and Indians. And there, he made Jedediah his partner.

It was a short-lived partnership. At the next summer's rendezvous, on the Bear River near Soda Springs (there had been an earlier rendezvous that summer in Cache Valley), Ashley announced that he had seen enough of the mountains; he would sell out and return to St. Louis. Jedediah Smith, the logical successor, formed a new partnership with David E. Jackson and William L. Sublette,

bought out Ashley's trade goods, and took command.

His new empire was huge, encompassing the Central Rockies, the vast Green and Bear River country, the canyons and valleys of the Wasatch. But it was not big enough for Jedediah. The British Hudson's Bay Company controlled trapping to the north and northwest, and the Crows and Shoshones made life there unhealthy anyway. New Mexican trappers were crowding into the Southern Rockies.

If a man wanted to expand—and Jedediah was nothing if not expansive—he had to look west and southwest. The Buenaventura River was out there somewhere, flowing from Utah or Great Salt Lake to the Pacific, and it had to be full of beaver. Besides, it was new country, and a man had to go see what he could see.

His own words tell what moved him. He hoped to "*find parts of the country as well stocked with Beaver as the waters of the Missouri which was as much as we could reasonably expect.*" But even more compelling was the unknown wilderness: "*In taking charge of our S western Expedition I followed the bent on my strong inclination to visit this unexplored country and unfold those hidden resources of wealth and bring to light those wonders which I readily imagined a country so extensive might contain . . . I wanted to be the first to view a country on which the eyes of a white man had never gazed and to follow the course of rivers that run through a new land.*"

So, almost before the ink had dried on his contract with Ashley, Jedediah was off on the first of two epic journeys. On the first, he would traverse Utah from north to south and then cross the entire Great Basin west to east—something that would take the combined efforts of such government-financed explorers as Fremont, Simpson, Stansbury, Gunnison, and Beckwith to accomplish during the next third century.

While he was gone, Jackson and Sublette, with most of the men, would trap up the Snake to the Teton country, then along the Gallatin and Yellowstone rivers and the headwaters of the Columbia. The partners would rendezvous the next summer at Bear Lake.

With eighteen men, Smith set out on August 7, moving south through the lava country of the Portneuf Valley, through Cache Valley, up Sardine Canyon, down Box Elder Canyon along the route of present-day Highway 89-91, through Salt Lake Valley to the Jordan River, and on to Utah Lake. He spent five or six days, probably August 21-26, among the Ute Indians at the lake, seeking information about the country to the south. He also concluded a peace treaty allowing Americans to trap and travel through the country—a treaty, one supposes, that would greatly benefit the Mormons a quarter-century later.

Jedediah found the Utes *"cleanly quiet and active and make a nearer approach to civilized life than any Indians I have seen in the Interior. Their leggings and shirts which are made of the skins of the Deer Mt Sheep or Antelope are kept quite clean."* More important, *"I found these Indians more honest than any I have been with in the country. They appear to have verry little dis-*

position to steal and ask for nothing unless it may be a little meat. As stealing and Begging are the most degrading features in the Indian character and as their prevalence is almost universal so to be exempt from them is no ordinary merit."

From Utah Lake, the easy and logical way was south along the base of the Wasatch and then up the Sevier River, the route he would take the following year. But there were no beaver that way, the Indians told him. The mountains to the east held beaver, they said. Besides, their chief, with whom Jedediah wanted to meet, was somewhere up there gathering serviceberries. And, like the bear going over the mountain, Smith had to see what he could see.

So, after buying three horses *"for which I paid a high price"*, the party headed east, probably up Spanish Fork Canyon, more or less along Escalante's route of a half-century earlier. Jedediah reported *"the country extremely rough until ascending a considerable Mt we kept on the top of a ridge running Eastwardly"*—probably Soldier Summit.

He descended to the Price River, found beaver there, and trapped a couple of days. Then he *"moved on South having a high range of Mountains on the West and crossing a good many small streams running East into a large valley the valley of the Colorado."* He had arrived at Castle Valley. The *"many small streams"* included Huntington, Cottonwood, Ferron, and Muddy creeks, all draining off the Wasatch Plateau, his *"high range of Mountains on the West."*

Anyone who has explored the naked rock

and deeply eroded canyons of the San Rafael Swell to the southeast will appreciate Smith's next entry: *"But having learned that the valley was verry barren and Rocky I did not venture into it . . . after traveling in this direction 2 days the country looked so unpromising that I determined to strike westward to a low place in the Mountain and cross over."*

The *"low place"* was apparently up Ivie Creek and over the pass to Salina Canyon. Jedediah's were not the first footprints made by white men here. Two Spanish traders, Arze and Garcia, probably came this way in 1813 while fleeing hostile Indians along the Sevier. There may have been others as well, and there would be many thousands to follow. This became the main Spanish Trail—and is now the route of I-70.

An important part of wilderness travel was making friends with the Indians, upon whom the trappers depended for guidance on the trails and for replenishing food supplies. Friendship also helped to preserve scalps. In Salina Canyon, Jedediah showed his skill:

"In crossing this mountain just as we were encamping I found an old squaw . . . one of the men gave her a Badger which I supposed she would take home to cook and eat. But the moment it was presented she caught it in her hands and exclaimed 'we are all friends' . . . and immediately tore it in pieces and laid it on the coals. When it was about half cooked she commenced eating making no nice distinction between hair pelts entrails and meet."

In three days Jedediah reached the Sevier River, which he named the Ashley *"in com-*

Site of first trappers' rendezvous on
Henrys Fork of the Green River
along the Utah-Wyoming border.
Uinta Mountains in background.
George Wuerthner

pliment to my friend the enterprising Genl.
W H Ashley.'' There were beaver sign, but
the trapping was disappointing. He described
the Indians with a fine eye for detail:

*"The Indians at this place are rather
above the midling size but in the mental
scale lower than any I have yet seen . . . they
are strongly contrasted with the cleanliness
of the Uta's . . . They appear to subsist
entirely on Roots . . .* [which] *they prepare
by laying them on heated Stones and covering them first with grass and then with earth
where they remain until they are sufficiently
steamed. They are then mashed fine and
made into small cakes.''*

As he moved south up the Sevier, noting
the large number of blacktailed hare that
would so impress later travelers, Jedediah was
impressed by another Indian practice:

*"They have a peculiar method of convey-
ing intelligence of the approach of danger.
Each family or set of families has a quantity of dry Sedge Bark and Brush piled up
near the habitation and immediately on the
approach of a Stranger they set fire to the
pile and this being seen by their neighbor he
does the same and the next the same so that
the alarm flies over the hills in every direction with the greatest rapidity.''*

Finding Marysvale Canyon pinching in on
the Sevier, Jedediah turned west up Clear
Creek and crossed the foothills of the Tushar
Mountains towering to the south. The route
he pioneered was a good one; I-70 follows
it today to its junction with I-15 at Cove Fort.

Here, Jedediah ran out of beaver and out
of real streams. Finding small streams coming out of the mountains, he followed them

west *"and was not a little surprised to find
that they all sunk in the sand.''*

*"On the following morning I started SW
we moved in that direction about 20 miles
and to my great Surprise instead of a River
an immense sand plain was before me where
the utmost view with my Glass could not
embrace any appearance of water. The only
exception to this interminable waste of sand
was a few detached rocky hills that rose from
the surrounding plain and the stunted sedge
that was thinly scattered over its surface.''*

He was looking out over the Escalante
Desert, the country that had turned the Spanish padres back fifty years earlier. And he was
learning something about the character of the
Great Basin. Later, he would learn much
more.

Staying close to the mountains on the east
because he could find water there, Jedediah
pushed on south, following today's route of
I-15 to the Beaver River. Here he made the
mistake of trying to follow the river west,
only to find it sinking in the sand; he named
it Lost River. Retracing steps, he then moved
through Parowan and Cedar Valley, passing
the future site of Cedar City, and on to the
rim of the Great Basin.

He started down Ash Creek between the
beautiful red rock scarps of the Hurricane
Cliffs on the left and the laccolithic Pine Valley Mountains soaring to the right. But this
route, which I-15 now follows, was too
rough. The trappers turned southwest and
found another way over Black Ridge, possibly along Cedar Ridge and down Quail
Creek.

On September 22, forty-six days from ren-

dezvous, Jedediah reached the confluence of
the Virgin and Santa Clara rivers. Here, where
condominiums now surround lush golf
courses in the St. George-Bloomington area,
Jedediah found *"no game or Beaver* [so] *we
had nothing to eat.''* But he did find *"a small
spot of ground where corn had been raised
3 or 4 years since. Some of my men could
hardly believe it possible that corn had ever
been planted in this lonely country . . .''*

They would soon believe, thanks to
Jedediah's skill in making friends with the
Indians. He wrote:

*"I had advanced a little ahead of the
company to look for a place to encamp, near
a small Creek* [the Santa Clara] *coming in
from the west and at the distance of 200
yards I observed an Indian on a hill and
made signs for him to come to me but he
presented his bow and arrows and in a
moment I saw 15 or 20 appear. not considering it safe to remain here I hastened
back to the party and then proceeded onto
the selected encampment. By this time 20 or
30 were seen skulking around among the
Rocks. I therefore had every thing prepared
for the worst and advancing alone before the
camp by making signs and speaking in a
friendly tone of voice I finally succeeded in
persuading one of them to come to me. The
poor fellow the bravest in the band advanced
with evident signs of fear his limbs trembling
and his voice faltering. holding out in his
hand a hare or rabbit to offer as a token of
friendship. I took it and carrassed him and
he immediately set down. When the others
saw that he was not hurt 10 or 12 of them
came bringing in their hands an ear of corn*

Above: North Stansbury Mountains. Jedediah Smith and his party found a life-saving spring here.
John George

Opposite: Evening light on the San Rafael River from the Wedge Overlook. After two days' travel toward the San Rafael Swell, Jedediah Smith wrote that "having learned that the valley was verry barren and Rocky I did not venture into it."
Scott T. Smith

as an emblem of peace - they set down Began to talk and make signs. As provisions was our greatest present desire we were much pleased to hear that they had corn and pumpkins close at hand."

The feast that followed, Smith wrote, was *"a treat that made my party in their sudden hilarity and Glee present a lively contrast to the moody desponding silence of the night before."*

The party stayed three days with these Indians, resting both men and horses and trading for a supply of corn. Jedediah was impressed by the Indians' pottery *"which is thiner than common Brown earthen colored yellow lead Color and like stone ware."* He also was intrigued by their pipes *"made of fine clouded marble,"* and obtained one to send to Indian Agent General William Clark.

Moving on, the party climbed a mesa to the right to get around the Virgin River Narrows, but they were soon blocked by a deep ravine. *". . . the descent was extremely steep,"* Jedediah wrote, *"and as we had no water since morning I was obliged to follow down the Ravine to the River & as it was then nearly night encamped without any grass for my horses."*

Now there was no avoiding the gorge. *"Early the next morning we started down in the bed of the general shallowness of the water. By the meanderings of the stream it was about 12 miles through the rocks rising perpendicularly from the waters edge in most places to the height of 3 or 400 feet . . . At one place I was obliged to unload and swim the horses."*

Jedediah would avoid the Narrows on his trip the following year. He found another way to the north, over Utah Hill, which the Spanish Trail would follow, and so would Highway 91. Except for later recreational hikers, few others would attempt the Narrows. A spectacularly designed freeway now fills this gorge, the most expensively-built section of freeway in the country.

The party pushed on past the Narrows to the Muddy and the Colorado, crossing that river above present-day Hoover Dam and heading straight south through difficult country to the Mojave villages at present-day Needles. The Spanish Trail would avoid that long swing south, shortcutting to Las Vegas and across southern Nevada to the Amargosa River.

Jedediah found the Mojaves to be friendly and hospitable. *"I was treated with great kindness,"* he wrote. *"Melons and roasted pumpkins were presented in great abundance."* This reception was in startling contrast to that of the following year, when most of his party would be slaughtered by Indians of this same tribe.

Smith now moved across the wide, arid valleys of southern California to the Mojave River and across the San Bernardino Mountains to the settlements, reaching the first one on November 25. He was apprehensive:

"It would perhaps be supposed that after numerous hardships endured in a savage and inhospitable desert I should hail the herds that were passing before me in the valley as harbingers of better times. But they reminded me that I was approaching a country inhabited by Spaniards. A people whose distinguishing characteristic has ever been jealousy a people of different religion from mine and possessing a full share of that bigotry and disregard of the rights of a Protestant that has at times tainted the Catholic Religion. They might perhaps consider me a spy imprison me persecute me for the sake of religion or detain me in prison to the ruin of my business . . . "

Detain them they did, though not in prison. Two months of entanglement in Spanish bureaucracy was almost as bad. It was late January before Jedediah again crossed the San Bernardino Mountains, and then under strict instructions to go back the way he had come. The Spaniards wanted no covetous-eyed Americans wandering through their country.

Jedediah interpreted his instructions loosely. He figured that once east of the San Bernardinos he was no longer in California. So, instead of heading back over the desert, he turned north along the edge of the Mojave and on to San Joaquin Valley. He would find the Buenaventura River and follow it back to Salt Lake Valley.

But there was no Buenaventura. Instead, he faced the fearsome wall of the Sierras. His men trapped the swift streams rushing down from those slopes, and by the first of May they had reached the American River with 1500 pounds of pelts. With the Indians becoming more numerous and troublesome, it was time to turn for home.

He hoped the snow would be hard enough to support a horse, but Smith would soon learn that it wasn't: *". . . in advancing the snow became deeper and less compact and when I had got about 12 miles from my encampment the horses began to sink so deep as to render the prospect of proceeding verry doubtful. we were not yet at the highest part of the Mt and the distances across was unknown. This was our situation when news came up from the rear that some of the horses had given out being able to proceed no further."*

Smith faced a dilemma that would try the most resourceful leader. Retracing their steps down the mountain, he wrote, would risk the lives of his men among hostile Indians, some of whom he had had to kill on the way up. And then what? Traveling farther north seemed useless; the mountains only grew higher. Returning to the missions in San Bernardino Valley was unthinkable.

In this crisis, Jedediah grew introspective: *"The sight in its extended range embraced no living being except it caught a transient glimpse of my little party awaiting my return in the snows below. It was indeed a freezing desolation and one which I thought should keep a man from wandering. I thought of home and all its neglected enjoyments of the cherful fireside of my father house of the Pleanteous harvest of my native land and visions of flowing fields of green and wide spread Prairaes of joyous bustle and of busy life thronged in my mind to make me feel more strongly the utter desolateness of my situation. And is it possible thought [I] that we are creatures of choice and that we follow fortune through such paths as these . . . "*

But he had to make a decision. The party would retrace their steps south as far as the Stanislaus River, where the Indians were friendlier. He would leave the bulk of the party there to trap and fend for themselves. With Silas Gobel and Robert Evans, he would make another attempt to cross the Sierras and then hurry on to the scheduled Bear Lake rendezvous. Then he would return to the Stanislaus with a stronger party. If he hadn't made it back by September 20, they were to consider him dead and make their own way home.

It didn't turn out quite that way. Jedediah would return by that date—by August 15, in fact—but with only six men, ten others of the rescue party having been murdered by the Mojaves. And when the reunited party did get organized and set out on the tortuous journey up the California and Oregon coasts, disaster would follow. All but six men would be massacred on the Umpqua River in southern Oregon. Jedediah, whose only means of supporting his expeditions was the harvesting of beaver pelts, would return from his two epic journeys with only the clothes on his back.

But that was yet to come. The challenge immediately ahead was to make white man's first crossing of the Sierras.

Smith, Gobel, and Evans set out up the Stanislaus on May 20 with six horses and two mules. They carried sixty pounds of dried meat and, remembering that they had lost five horses to starvation in the first attempt to cross the mountains, hay to feed the horses.

It was a terrible ordeal. A storm caught them on the fifth day out. Jedediah described it:

"The Storm still continued with unabated violence. I was obliged to remain in camp.

It was one of the most disagreeable days I ever passed . . . The wind was continually changing and the snow drifting and flying in every direction. It was with great difficulty that we could get wood and we were but just able to keep our fire. Our poor animals felt a full share of the vengeance of the storm and 2 horses and one mule froze to death before our eyes . . . It seemed that we were marked out for destruction and that the sun of another day might never rise to us. But He that rules the Storms willed it otherwise and the sun of the 27th rose clear uppon the gleaming peaks . . . "

After five more days of struggling over Ebbetts Pass and down the east slopes of the Sierras, Jedediah reached Walker Lake. Fremont would discover this lake in 1845 and name it for his guide, Joe Walker. But Smith was the first American to camp on its shores, eighteen years earlier.

The journey across Nevada more or less followed the route of present-day U.S. 50-6, which is still called *"the loneliest highway in America."* Jedediah described the country as mostly barren and destitute, often leaving them without water for two days at a time, and inhabited by naked Indians *"who appeared the most miserable of the human race having nothing to subsist on except grass seed, grasshoppers, &c."*

On June 20, the three men entered Utah after crossing the Snake Mountains north of Wheeler Peak, through Sacramento Pass where Highway 50-6 now runs. Turning north through Snake Valley, they were caught in the bogs of Salt Marsh Lake. One horse was so hopelessly mired, they killed it and took a quarter for meat.

Jedediah thought little of this country or its inhabitants, describing the Gosiutes they encountered as *"nearly naked having at*

most a scanty robe formed from the skin of the hare peculiar to this plain which is cut into narrow strips and interwoven with a kind of twine or cord made apparently from wild flax or hemp. They form a connecting link between the animal and intelectual creation and quite in keeping with the country in which they are located."

Keeping the snow-covered peaks of the Deep Creek Mountains on their left, the three trudged on to the vicinity of Fish Springs. *"The Country so much resembled that on the south side of the Salt Lake,"* Jedediah wrote, *"that for a while I was induced to believe that I was near that place."* But he wasn't. Some of the most painful of all his travels remained before he would reach there.

They pushed now into the southern tip of the Great Salt Lake desert and camped without water or grass. The next morning, Jedediah wrote, *"I started verry early in*

hopes of soon finding water. But ascending a high point of a hill [in the Dugway Range] *I could discover nothing but sandy plains or dry Rocky hills with the Exception of a snowy mountain off to the NE at a distance of 50 or 60 Miles.* [Deseret Peak in the Stansbury Range] *When I came down I durst not tell my men of the desolate prospect ahead, but framed my story so as to discourage them as little as possible . . . But the view ahead was almost hopeless. With our best exertion we pushed forward walking as we had been for a long time over the soft sand. That kind of traveling is verry tiresome to men in good health who can eat when and what they choose and drink as often as they desire, and to us worn down with hunger and fatigue and burning with thirst increased by the blazing sands it was almost insuportable."*

Resting when they could go no farther, digging holes in the sand to escape the blaz-

ing sun, they struggled on. They traveled all that night, and were deep within what is now the Dugway Proving Grounds. Jedediah continued:

"June 25 When morning came it saw us in the same unhappy situation pursuing our journey over the desolate waste now gleming in the sun and more insuportably tormenting than it had been during the night. At 10 O Clock Robert Evans laid down in the plain under the shade of a small cedar being able to proceed no further. The Mountain of which I have before spoken was apparently not far off and we left him and proceeded onward in the hope of finding water in time to return with some in season to save his life. After traveling about three Miles we came to the foot of the Mt and then to our inexpressible joy we found water. Goble plunged into it at once and I could hardly wait to bath my burning forehead

before I was pouring it down regardless of the consequence . . . "

This life-giving spring was probably at the foot of the Stansburys, at the western edge of Skull Valley. From it, they took water back to Evans.

And now, the ordeal was over. In two days, they reached the north end of the Stansburys. *"The Salt Lake a joyful sight was spread before us,"* Smith wrote. *"Is it possible said the companions of my sufferings that we are so near the end of our troubles . . . It was indeed a most cheering view for although we were some distance from the depo yet we knew we would soon be in a country where we would find game and water which were to us objects of the greatest importance and those which would contribute more than any others to our comfort and happiness. Those who may chance to read this at a distance from the scene may*

Autumn in central Utah near Jedediah Smith's route along the Sevier River
Jeff Gnass

Sunset, Bear River marshes
John George

perhaps be surprised that the sight of this lake surrounded by a wilderness of more than 2000 miles diameter excited in me these feelings known to the traveler who after long and perilous journeying comes again in view of his home. But so it was with me for I had traveled so much in the vicinity of the Salt Lake that it had become my home of the wilderness.''

It took a day of travel along the south shore of the lake to reach the flood-swollen Jordan River, which nearly drowned the three men as they tried to pull a raft across. But that was a small inconvenience. Hunger was a greater one, and here they ate the last of the horse meat. But the next day, in Salt Lake Valley, Jedediah shot a fat buck and soon had the meat cooking.

"We then employed ourselves most pleasantly in eating for about two hours and for the time being forgot that we were not the happiest people in the world . . . "

Two more days brought them to their cache on Blacksmiths Fork in Cache Valley, where they learned from Indians that the rendezvous was assembled on the south shore of Bear Lake.

Smith's final entry for this historic trek: *"I hired a horse and a guide and at three O Clock arrived at the rendezvous. My arrival caused a considerable bustle in camp for myself and party had been given up as lost. A small Cannon brought up from St Louis* [the first wheeled vehicle to cross South Pass] *was loaded and fired for a salute.''*

That was July 3. Incredibly, on July 13 he

was on his way again. With eighteen men, he set out to retrace his route [except that this time he would avoid the detour into Castle Valley] all the way back to his men waiting on the Stanislaus. The expedition would be a disaster, with the killing of most of his men by the Mojaves before he reached the Stanislaus party, and the killing of most of that party on the way up the Oregon Coast. Such disaster would ruin a lesser man.

But Jedediah was nothing if not resilient. After another year of trapping, he was able to send his brother $2,200 for his parents, a Dr. Simon, and for the brother himself. In the letter of instructions, he summarized his career in the mountains. His rationalization may seem a bit forced, coming from a man who so obviously explored for the love of it. But the character of the man shines through:

"It is that I may be able to help those who stand in need, that I face every danger—it is for this, that I traverse the Mountains covered with eternal Snow—it is for this that I pass over the Sandy Plains, in heat of Summer, thirsting for water, and am well pleased if I can find a shade, instead of water, where I may cool my overheated Body—it is for this that I go for days without eating, & am pretty well satisfied if I can gather a few roots, a few Snails, or, much better Satisfied if we can afford our selves a piece of Horse Flesh, or a fine roasted Dog, and, most of all, it is for this, that I deprive myself of the privilege of Society & the satisfaction of the Converse of My Friends!''

Sunset, Windowblind Peak, San Rafael Swell. Calling it "sandy, hilly & utterly barren," *one traveler on the Spanish Trail wrote,* "I can hardly conceive of what earthly use a large proportion of this country was designed for."
Tom Till

OLD SPANISH TRAIL

It was the longest, crookedest, toughest pack trail in North America, if not the world. For 1,200 miles, it wound from Santa Fe through southwestern Colorado into Utah, looped in a great northern arc from the southeast to the southwest corner of Utah, touched a corner of Arizona, and crossed the waterless wastes of southern Nevada and southern California to Los Angeles.

More than a third of it—450 miles—and most of its variety, from sagebrush plains to high mountain passes to deep redrock canyons, lay in Utah. It was in Utah that the trail crossed the only major rivers on the route, the Colorado and the Green.

It was a trading trail, and Utah produced one of the trading commodities—Indian slaves. But the major commodity was horses and mules from the lush ranches of southern California. Uncounted thousands of animals, traded for New Mexican woolen blankets, or stolen, trailed over those long, dusty miles for sale in New Mexico or on east over the Santa Fe Trail to markets in Missouri. For twenty years, during the 1830s and 1840s, that trade pounded hoofprints deep into western soil.

History calls it the Old Spanish Trail, which is appropriate only because the New World Spaniards first conceived of such a trail to tie together their widely scattered empire. They never forged the link, even after investing untold energy, enterprise, and courage into building such an empire.

A previous chapter has described New Spain's establishment of missions along the California coast and in New Mexico, and the efforts of Father Garces and Fathers Dominguez and Escalante to open a trail from Santa Fe to California. They failed. When a trail did finally evolve, along a different route, no Spaniard ever traveled its length. Not until after Mexico had won its independence from Spain in 1821 were the energies unlocked that pushed the trail through. By then, religious missionary zeal was no longer the incentive; the lure of private profits was the motivating force.

That lure was there, of course, long before Mexican independence. As early as 1716, in an expedition against the Utes in southern Colorado, the Spanish had discovered the profit in selling captured Indians as slaves. Quick learners, the Utes entered the slave trade themselves, and for the next century Spanish traders from New Mexico penetrated Ute country in western Colorado and Utah, trading horses, knives, and blankets for furs and slaves.

Documents on such trade are few, but two important expeditions are recorded. In 1805, Manuel Mestas, at age seventy, led an expedition from Santa Fe to the Timpanogos Indians whom Escalante had visited at Utah Lake twenty-nine years earlier. In 1813, Mauricio Arze and Lagos Garcia also reached Utah Lake, then traveled south along the Sevier River until they encountered a hostile band of Indians and fled for their lives east to the Colorado. Both expeditions undoubtedly followed part of what became the Spanish Trail. In their flight from the Sevier, Arze and Garcia may have crossed the Wasatch Plateau along the route the Spanish Trail later followed through Salina Canyon. They returned with twelve Indian slaves and 109 pelts, lamenting that these were *"but a few."* Evidently, unrecorded earlier expeditions had been more successful.

In their seminal work, *Old Spanish Trail*, LeRoy and Ann Hafen outlined how, step by step, the trail might have been developed. Escalante had gone far north through western Colorado, entering Utah near present-day Vernal and traversing the Uintah Basin to cross the Wasatch Mountains to Utah Lake via Spanish Fork Canyon. Mestas and other traders would have no reason to make this long detour. More likely, they followed the Gunnison River to its junction with the Colorado, followed the Colorado to where it swings south at about the Utah state line and, then struck due west to the Green River. The only feasible crossing is near the present-day town of Green River. To the north the Green flows deep in the forbidding Gray and Desolation Canyons, to the south in Labyrinth Canyon. From this crossing, traders would have followed the Price River to its head, then down Spanish Fork River to Utah Lake.

The next big shortcut would enter Utah south of the La Sal Mountains to a crossing of the Colorado near present-day Moab, then on to the Green River crossing. And the next would eliminate the long northern loop to Utah Lake by striking west from Green River through the San Rafael Swell to Castle Valley, then over the Wasatch Plateau to the Sevier River via Salina Canyon.

Modern backpackers in the magnificently rugged San Rafael country will readily understand this Hafen paragraph:

"It is not likely that this trail through difficult country was finally worked out

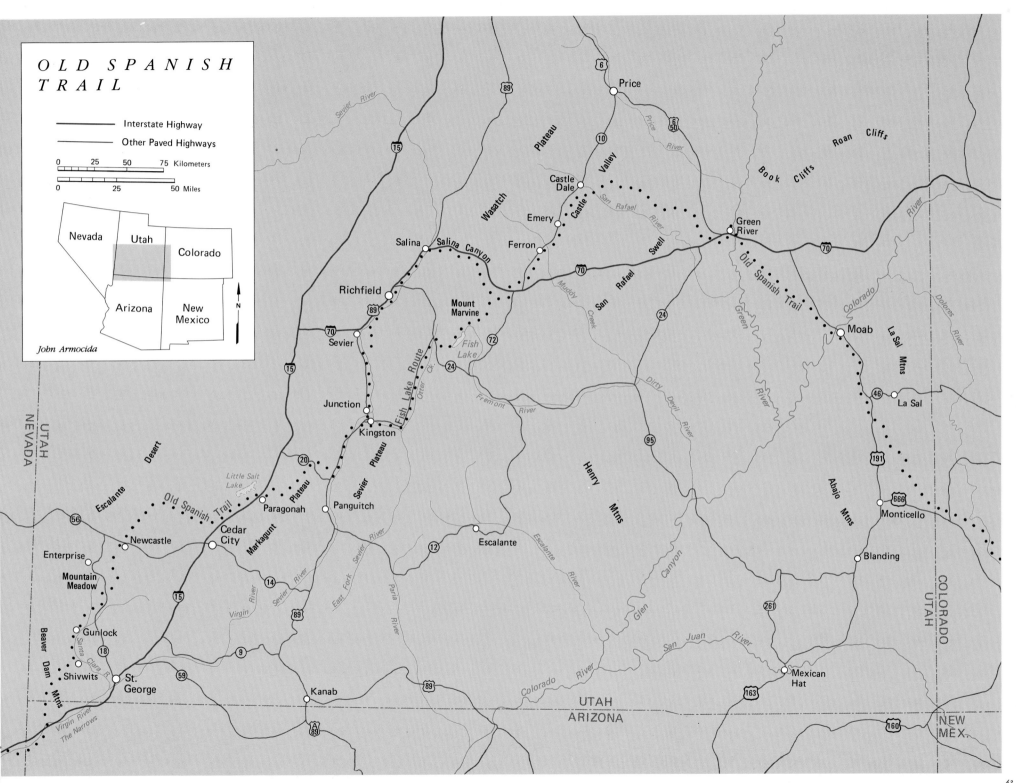

OLD SPANISH TRAIL

Interstate Highway
Other Paved Highways

0   25   50   75 Kilometers
0   25   50 Miles

Nevada   Utah   Colorado
Arizona   New Mexico

N

John Armocida

without explorers first suffering tragic experiences with the Dirty Devil and San Rafael. Both streams flow in the general direction that homeward-bound New Mexicans would naturally be inclined to take. But both lead into such rugged country and such deep, forbidding canyons, that anyone who attempted to descend them to their denouements into the Colorado and Green Rivers respectively, would not again endure the ordeal."

Thus, the Spanish Trail evolved. Escalante had blazed it from Santa Fe to the Utah-Colorado border, Garces from Los Angeles to the Mojave villages at the southern tip of Nevada. But what of the vast stretch between? No one knows just how or when or by which Santa Fe trader each segment and shortcut of the trail was developed through the eastern half of Utah.

But there's no doubt about the part through southwestern Utah. In the history of western exploration, no name is written bolder than that of Jedediah Smith. In his two historic treks from the Cache Valley and Bear Lake regions to Los Angeles in 1826 and 1827, he linked the trails established by Garces and Escalante fifty years earlier. Other Mountain Men followed over parts of the trail in the next few years—-Americans like Daniel Potts, Ewing Young, Kit Carson, Pegleg Smith, and even a Britisher, Peter Skene Ogden. The trail as it finally took shape differed in places from Jedediah's trace, but still he stands alone as the principal pathfinder through southwestern Utah.

A look at a map of the Old Spanish Trail raises the question: How did Utah become

part of it at all? Why the great northern loop through Utah, which added more than 200 miles to the trail's length? Why not follow the logical east-west route from Santa Fe directly across northern New Mexico and Arizona to southern California?

Part of the answer lies in geography. That route is hotter, drier, and more deeply carved with the gorges of the Colorado drainage than the northern route. Especially drier. In 1829, a trapping party led by Ewing Young undertook to reach California by striking west from central Arizona. In the party was the young Kit Carson. His autobiography graphically describes why others preferred to swing north:

"The first four days' march was over a country, sandy, burned up, and without a drop of water. Each night we received a small quantity of water from the tanks [fashioned of deer hides] *which we had been foresighted enough to provide. A guard was placed over them to prohibit anyone from making use of more than his due allowance.*

"After four days' travel we found water. Before we reached it, the pack mules were strung along the road for several miles. They smelled the water long before we had any hopes of finding any, and all made the best use of the strength left them after their severe sufferings to reach it as soon as they could . . .

"After remaining in camp two days we resumed our expedition and for four days traveled over a country similar . . . There was no water to be found during this time, and we suffered extremely on account of it . . . "

So thirst was a persuasive reason to avoid the southern route. An even more compelling reason was fear of hostile Indians. Escalante had warned about that after his 1775 expedition to the Hopi villages in northern Arizona found the Indians sullen and inhospitable. Garces found them even more so the following year. Three years later, Garces learned about hostility in the ultimate way when he visited the missions he had founded among the Yuma villages and was killed along with his three companions and a number of settlers and soldiers. Other massacres followed, including that of the Jedediah Smith party at the Mojave villages on the Colorado in 1827. Plainly, the Indians of the desert had had their fill of white men.

By contrast, Escalante had found the various tribes who ranged the country north of the Colorado to be entirely friendly and helpful. That would change through the years, as the murdered Gunnison party and others were later to prove. But as the Spanish Trail was being opened, relations between whites and Indians were still good.

So through Utah the trail would go. By 1830, the separate efforts of Spanish priests, Mexican traders, and American fur trappers had prepared the way. In that year, twenty trappers led by William Wolfskill and George C. Yount were the first to travel the entire length of what became, from the time of their journey, the Old Spanish Trail. It took experience to make such a trip, and the two leaders qualified. Wolfskill had trapped and traded horses out of Santa Fe for eight years. Yount had trapped along the Colorado for four, making two trips to the Mojave villages and one to Utah Lake during that time.

The partnership they formed in 1830 was to trap for beaver along the way to and in California. As it turned out, in their eagerness to reach California they did little trapping en route. Once there, the party broke up. Yount, Wolfskill, and Ziba Branch became prominent California citizens; most of the others vanished from history, leaving no mark except the distinction of being the first to travel the length of the Spanish Trail.

Later reminiscences give some flavor of the trek and an indication of the route. Having crossed the Green River, Yount recalled, they *"passed over an extremity of mountainous and barren territory"* before they *"struck a ravine which led them directly to the Revere [Sevier] river."* This was the rugged passage through the north end of the San Rafael Swell, the long, dry trek across Buckhorn Flat to Castle Valley, then the crossing of the Wasatch Plateau by way of Salina Canyon.

On the Sevier they found the Ute Indians mourning the death of their chief. The trappers witnessed the funeral pyre, smoked the peace pipe, gave presents of beads, tobacco, and knives, and received formal permission to travel and trap through the Indian lands.

Pushing up the Sevier, they missed the right turn Jedediah Smith had taken up Clear Creek for an easy passage between the Pavant and Tushar mountains to level country near Cove Fort—the present route of I-70. Farther on, they also missed what would become the regular Spanish Trail route up Bear Creek and down Red Creek to present-day Paragonah.

As Yount later recalled, that mistake got them into deep trouble:

"Our trappers, with much toil, reached a strip of Table land, upon a lofty range of mountains [apparently the 9,000-foot Markagunt Plateau above Panguitch], where they encountered the most terrible snowstorm they had ever experienced. During several days, no one ventured out of camp. There they lay embedded in snow, very deep, animals and men huddled thick as possible together, to husband and enjoy all possible animal warmth, having spread their thick and heavy blankets, & piled bark and brush wood around & over them . . . After the storm subsided and the weather had softened, Yount & Wolfskill ascended a lofty Peak of the mountains for observation. In the whole range of human view, in every direction, nothing could be discerned, in the least degree encouraging, but only mountains, piled on mountains, all capped with cheerless snow, in long and continuous succession, till they seemed to mingle with the blue vault of heaven and fade away in the distance. It was a cheerless prospect . . . This was all they had learned by the laborious ascent up the Mountain Peak. Several of their animals had perished in the piercing cold . . .

"The reader must imagine the journey from this lofty station to Virgin River Valley, for words are poor things to describe it; neither can words describe the feelings & emotions, which struggled in the breasts of the party, while there encamped, & when groping their way upon the glare ice, & frozen snow, down the steep declivities &

into the vallies which lie beneath them . . ."

But Utah is nothing if not diversity, as the party soon learned: *"After a few days march, they knew not whither, & what to hope for, to their utter astonishment, they were ushered into another of those enchanting vallies. There the earth was bare of snow, & the evergreens waved in gentleness and calm serenity. The Elk, deer and antelope, driven from the mountains, by the snow & piercing cold, were basking, with their frolicsome fawns, unaware & unintimidated by the sight of man. They would flock around like domestic sheep or goats . . ."*

The location of this *"enchanting valley"* is hard to pin down. It does not seem to be where the party emerged from the mountains, at the Little Salt Lake near Paragonah, since at that place they were forced to kill the last of the four beeves they had driven from New Mexico. Nor does it seem to have come later, since Yount wrote that from here on it was horse and mule meat and short allowance, which, one member of the party recalled, *"was very poor."*

Pushing south along Jedediah Smith's trail, the trappers reached the Virgin River and descended it to the Colorado, which they followed south to the Mojave villages near present-day Needles, California. From there, they struck west across the Mojave Desert. Yount vividly remembered the last section of the trail in Utah: *"The soil is red sandstone & therefore the waters of the [Virgin] River are almost like blood."*

Traders following the trail after 1830 developed some important variations. One was a shorter but higher alternate to the trail

Petrified dunes in Arches National Park and the La Sal Mountains on the horizon. Travelers on the Spanish Trail beheld this view more than a century and a half ago.
Jeff Gnass

through Salina Canyon; it wound around the south end of Fish Lake and down Otter Creek to rejoin the trail on the Sevier at present-day Kingston. Another left the Jedediah Smith trail at Summit north of present-day Cedar City, struck west through the Escalante Desert to Newcastle, south to Mountain Meadow, then down the Santa Clara River to its junction with the Virgin. A third avoided the treacherous Indians at Mojave by leaving the Virgin-Colorado route at the southwest corner of Utah and striking west across southern Nevada to enter California south of Death Valley. Many thirsty miles lay between waterholes on that route, and bleached bones soon littered the trail. But it was shorter and, for people, safer.

For a quarter-century after the Yount-Wolfskill passage, the Spanish Trail saw a strange and diverse succession of travelers. Trappers followed parts of it during the early period, and gold-seeking Forty Niners followed it later. There were discontents seeking new homes in California, slavers, horse thieves, military expeditions, adventurers. But by far the greatest volume of traffic was by traders.

As the supply of and market for beavers declined, some Mountain Men turned to trade, packing out loads of dressed deerskins from the Ute Indian country and returning with droves of horses and mules to sell to the Utah Mormon settlements. Far more trade was of blankets from the high sheep country of New Mexico. Long mule trains carried bales of woolen goods to exchange for the horses and mules that could be bought for a dollar or less in California and sold for twenty times that amount in New Mexico.

Seldom has supply more dramatically exceeded demand. In their earliest years, the California missions barely survived starvation. Forty years later, horses had multiplied so greatly on the lush grasslands that they had to be slaughtered by the thousands. An early rancher, Jose del Carmen Lugo, recalled that wild horses had become so troublesome during the early 1820s that the pueblo of Los Angeles organized a killing program.

"I remember seeing three corrals for this purpose here in Los Angeles," he wrote. *"Cowboys, on horseback, drove whole herds of wild and tame animals into these enclosures and closed the great gates. There were some small gates, through which only one horse could pass at a time. Two or three lancers were stationed at each of these gates to spear the wild horses as they emerged, this being done after the ranchers had indicated the animals they were claiming. The slaughter of wild horses continued until none but the animals that had been claimed were left in the corrals. Many thousands of horses were slaughtered in these times . . . "*

How many horses were bought and trailed east across the Spanish Trail will never be known, since few records were kept. It must have been tens of thousands. One caravan crossed Cajon Pass with 4150 legally acquired horses. Others typically drove half that many, but the caravans were huge. A French observer, Duflot de Mofras, described the traffic in 1841:

"Caravans travel once a year from New Mexico to Los Angeles. These consist of 200 men on horseback, accompanied by mules laden with fabrics and large woollen covers called serapes, jerzas, and cobertones, which are valued at 3 to 5 piasters each. This merchandise is exchanged for horses and mules, on a basis, usually, of two blankets for one animal. Caravans leave Santa Fe, New Mexico, in October, before the snows set in . . . and finally reach the outlying ranchos of California from where the trail leads into El Pueblo de los Angeles. This trip consumes two and one-half months. Returning caravans leave California in April in order to cross the rivers before the snow melts, taking with them about 2,000 horses. The expedition that reached El Pueblo in November, 1841, included in addition to some 200 New Mexicans, 60 or more North Americans."

Lieutenant George D. Brewerton, traveling with Kit Carson in 1848, described a caravan they passed on the way east:

"Their appearance was grotesque in the extreme. Imagine upward of two hundred Mexicans dressed in every variety of costume, from the embroidered jacket of the wealthy Californian, with its silver bell-shaped buttons, to the scanty habiliments of the skin-clad Indian, and you may form some idea of their dress. . . .The line of march of this strange cavalcade occupied an extent of more than a mile and I could not help thinking while observing their arms and equipments, that a few resolute men might have captured their property, and driven the traders like a flock of sheep . . . Near this motley crowd we sojourned for one night; and passing through their camp after dark, I was struck with its picturesque appearance. Their pack-saddles and bales had been taken off and carefully piled, so as not only to protect them from damp, but to form a sort of barricade or fort for their owner. From one side to the other of these little corrals of goods a Mexican blanket was stretched, under which the trader lay smoking his cigarrito, while his Mexican servant or slave—for they are little better—prepared his coffee and atole."

Little is known about the numbers of horses bought and driven legally from California, but even less is known about the numbers stolen. The raids started as early as 1829, when notorious Mountain Man Pegleg Smith ran off three or four hundred horses. From then until well into the 1850s, New Mexican traders, American trappers, and, finally, Ute Indians preyed regularly on the ranchos. By 1833, raids had become so alarming that Alcalde Carrillo of Los Angeles, in reporting the theft of 1,000 animals, mostly the more valuable mules, predicted that *"If the matter is not checked soon everything in the country will be taken away by the robbers."*

Utah-based trappers were deeply involved. In January 1840, fur trader Robert Newell wrote in his diary from Browns Hole on the Green River that with the fur trade drying up, the trappers had turned to horse thievery and that *"about 10 or 15 have gone to California for the purpose of Robbing and Steeling."* They must have been busy. That year saw the most spectacular

Yellow Bee plant, Beckwith Plateau near Green River along the Spanish Trail
John George

robberies of the entire period.

In May, thieves struck almost simultaneously at ranchos as widely scattered as Los Angeles, San Bernardino and San Juan Capistrano. Shortly after, Pegleg Smith and Ute Indian chief Wakara hit the mission of San Luis Obispo and drove off 1,200 horses and mules.

More than 3000 animals were rounded up and started east by some thirty men, including Smith, Wakara, Old Bill Williams, and Phil Thompson. The Californians determined that this time the thieves would not get away. Three separate posses, more than 100 men, set out in pursuit. They had little success. At a waterhole in the Mojave Desert, the Mountain Men ambushed the advance party of thirty men, drove off their mounts, and left them afoot. The rest of the pursuers caught up at Resting Spring, near the Nevada line, but by that time their mounts were jaded and the Mexicans had little taste for facing the trappers' rifles.

According to stories later told around the campfires, the Americans waited three days for an attack that did not come. Then, tired of inaction, they stole into the Mexican camp and drove off every horse and mule. That ended the pursuit. By that time, heat and thirst had killed half the stolen animals, but enough survived the rest of the trip to give the raiders a handsome profit

as well as bragging rights.

Others involved in horse stealing included the famous Mountain Men Joe Walker and James P. Beckwourth. Edwin Bryant, leading a small band of California-bound emigrants, ran into Walker at Fort Bridger in July 1846 and reported: *"He is driving some four or five hundred California horses, which he intends to dispose of in the United States. They appear to be high-spirited animals, of medium size, handsome figures, and in good condition."*

Beckwourth boasted that when the Mexican War broke out in 1846, *"considering all things fair in time of war, I, together with five trusty Americans, collected eighteen hundred stray horses we found roaming on the Californian ranchos, and started with our utmost speed from Pueblo de Angeles . . . We knew we should be pursued, and we lost no time in making our way toward home. We kept our herd jogging for five days and nights, only resting once a day to eat, and afford the animals time to crop a mouthful of grass . . . "*

When the Mexican War ended, California was in American hands and the Mountain Men stopped their raids. *"I never make war on my own people,"* Pegleg Smith explained. *"In driving off Spanish horses I might be brought in contact with my own countrymen, and you know that would not by any*

manner of means do." Besides, by that time he had plenty of horses for his ranch on the Bear River, from which in 1848 and 1849 he traded with the new Mormon settlement on Great Salt Lake.

He and his fellow American trappers may have had qualms about raids on American territory, but the Ute Indians didn't. Chief Wakara continued his forays despite Mormon efforts, in both California and Utah, to stop him. Company C of the Mormon Battalion was stationed at Cajon Pass in April 1847 to *"prevent a passage of hostile Indians with or without horses"* and to pursue and kill any they found. One such pursuit ended with six Indians killed and two troopers wounded.

In September 1848, Parley P. Pratt reported that Wakara was in Salt Lake City with several hundred horses for sale. In December that year, George A. Smith wrote:

"Walker [Wakara], the famous Utah chief has visited the Saints in the valley with his band of riflemen. He said he always wished to live in peace with our people; that his people should not steal from ours, if any of them did, let him know it and he would punish them and stop it. The brethren told him they did not want his men to steal from the Spaniards, for we were at peace with them. Walker replied: 'My men hate the Spaniards, they will steal from them and I cannot help it.' "

His statement was prophetic. Raids continued until 1853, when the Utes started raiding Mormon settlements in Utah, resulting in the Walker War.

Part of the reason for that war was the Mormon effort to stop another lucrative Ute business—the trading of Indian children as slaves to Mexican traders. In his book, *Forty Years Among the Indians*, Daniel W. Jones gave a horrifying account of this dispute:

"Stopping this slave business helped to sour some of Walker's band. They were in the habit of raiding on the Pahutes and low tribes, taking their children prisoners and selling them. Next year when they came up and camped on the Provo bench, they had some Indian children for sale. They offered them to the Mormons who declined buying. Arapine, Walker's brother, became enraged saying that the Mormons had stopped the Mexicans from buying these children; that they had no right to do so, unless they bought them themselves. Several of us were present when he took one of these children by the heels and dashed its brains out on the hard ground, after which he threw the body towards us, telling us we had no hearts, or we would have bought it and saved its life . . . "

What the Mormons were trying to stop was a trade that had existed, in one form or another, almost since the Spaniards arrived in the New World three and a half centuries earlier. It had existed for half a century in the area of the Old Spanish Trail and was one of the factors in establishing the trail. Jones described how the trade worked by 1850. Traders would set out from New Mexico with a few trade goods, he wrote, and trade with Navajos or Utes for a few horses.

"These used-up horses were brought through and traded to the poorer Indians for children. The horses were often used for food. This trading was continued into Lower California, where the children bought on the down trip would be traded to the Mexican-Californians for other horses, goods or cash. Many times a small outfit on the start would return with large herds of California stock.

"All children bought on the return trip would be taken back to New Mexico and then sold, boys fetching on an average $100, girls from $150 to $200. The girls were in demand to bring up for house servants, having the reputation of making better servants than any others. This slave trade gave rise to the cruel wars between the native tribes of this country, from Salt Lake down to the tribes in southern Utah. Walker and his band raided on the weak tribes, taking their children prisoners and selling them to the Mexicans. Many of the lower classes, inhabiting the southern deserts, would sell their own children for a horse and kill and eat the horse. The Mexicans were as fully established and systematic in this trade as ever were the slavers on the seas and to them it was a very lucrative business."

In 1852, the Utah legislature passed a law forbidding the slave trade, but the practice died hard. John D. Lee reported to the *Deseret News* in 1853 that Wakara had led a slave raid in southern Utah in which twenty men were killed or wounded and about that many women and children captured. Shortly after he arrived as a missionary to the Indians in southern Utah, Jacob Hamblin reported on the purchase of three girls by Sanpitch, Wakara's brother. As late as 1860, the federally appointed Indian Agent in Utah reported that the practice of taking slaves was still going on. *"Scarcely one-half of the Py-eed* [Piute] *children are permitted to grow up in the band,"* he reported, *"and a large majority of these being males, this and other causes are tending to depopulate their bands very rapidly."*

By that time, slavery no longer put traffic on the Old Spanish Trail; it had become mostly an Indian matter—Utes capturing Piutes to sell to Navajos. Pack mule caravans no longer kicked dust on the trail, nor did the great caballados of east-bound horses. Wagon wheels now rolled the long miles to Los Angeles. As a pack route, the Old Spanish Trail had become part of history.

Evening clouds, Fishlake National Forest. A branch of the Spanish Trail crossed these mountains.
John George

To relive the Old Spanish Trail, there's probably no better place than Emigrant Pass, near the California-Nevada border south of Death Valley. Here, the trail crossed the barren Nopah (no water) Mountains before dropping down to Resting Spring, the last good waterhole before the eighty-mile jornada del muerte (journey of death) to the Mojave River.

Harry Godshall, a retired dentist from Los Angeles, raises ornamental palms and blooded Arabian horses at Resting Springs. Atop Emigrant Pass, he led us along ruts of the old wagon road that Mormon guide Jefferson Hunt opened from Great Salt Lake to Los Angeles in 1849. Two hundred yards to the north, a sharply defined trail slashes across the volcanic ridge, deeply etched by the hooves of uncounted thousands of horses single-filing their way along the Spanish Trail toward Santa Fe. Both trails are plainly visible, snaking for miles across the broad and desolate Pahrump Valley to the east.

Unfortunately, we found no such tracks in Utah. A few dim traces can be found in the rocky hills just east of Castle Valley. Highway builders, plowing farmers, and more than a century of wind and water have left little else. Still, the route of the trail is well established. Motorists can follow much of it on modern highways. Hikers, mountain bikers, and four-wheelers can find adventure and a lively sense of how it must have been by searching out the off-highway sections.

Five men and a woman are primarily responsible for our knowledge of the trail through Utah. Three of the men made history in the nineteenth century. Two of them and

the woman wrote about it in the twentieth.

The first was John C. Fremont. In 1844, on the second of his five historic expeditions to the West, he followed the Spanish Trail from the Mojave River across the California and Nevada wastes to the Virgin—"The most dreary river I have ever seen," he wrote—then northeast to present-day Paragonah. Here, where the trail swings east, Fremont left it to follow the base of the Wasatch Plateau north to Utah Lake. His journal contains the best description of the western part of the trail through Utah.

For the eastern part, the search for a railroad route to California created maps and descriptions of the trail. Under orders of the Secretary of War, Captain J. W. Gunnison with thirty-two soldiers and seven surveyors followed the north branch of the Spanish Trail into Utah in 1853. Descending the Colorado to the vicinity of Cisco, Utah, that branch struck west along the route of I-70 to the crossing of the Green River, three miles upstream from the town of that name. Gunnison quickly concluded that no railroad could be built along the Spanish Trail through the San Rafael Swell, so took his eighteen wagons north almost to Price, then back south along the route of Highway 10 to rejoin the trail near Castle Dale. From there he followed the trail over the Wasatch by way of Salina Canyon, then left it to push west to what would become a date with disaster. On October 26, on the banks of the Sevier River southwest of present-day Delta, he and six of his men were murdered by Indians, their bodies left unburied to be picked clean by wolves.

Captain J.N. Macomb led an expe-

dition in 1859 to survey for a military wagon route. Macomb's party followed the main branch of the Spanish Trail into Utah south of the La Sal Mountains and across Lisbon Valley, then left the trail to explore the red-rock country to the west. That took them into canyon country where, they soon learned, no road could possibly be built. Macomb reported finding the confluence of the Green and Colorado rivers, and the map produced by the expedition was the first to show its approximate location. After years of research and field work, Moab historian Fran Barnes is convinced that Macomb was confused by the labyrinth of canyons and got no closer than eight miles from the confluence. Still, Macomb rates a place in Utah history as the first white man known to have penetrated what is now Canyonlands National Park. His and Gunnison's official maps and records documented important parts of the Spanish Trail.

Among modern histories of the trail, by far the most useful is the work of LeRoy and Ann Hafen, Old Spanish Trail, published in 1954 as part of their remarkable fifteen-volume "Far West and the Rockies" series. Their work brought together a rich lode of original source material, much of which is quoted in this chapter.

For the follower of trails, the other important work is that of Gregory C. Crampton, long-time historian at the University of Utah, now living and writing in St. George. His strip maps and description of the trail through Utah, printed in the Fall 1979 Utah Historical Quarterly, provide a reliable and insightful guide.

The main trail entered Utah directly

east of Monticello, near present-day Ucolo, swung northwest across the flats of the Great Sage Plains, now covered with dry-land farms, to the head of East Canyon. Here began one of the toughest sections of the entire trip, the trail dropping 1,000 feet in nine miles through a wildly twisted redrock gorge. Orville Pratt, a lawyer traveling to California under military orders with an eighteen-man escort, described his travels over this section on September 13, 1848:

"The mountains all about us [the great laccolith peaks of the Abajos to the west, the La Sals to the north] are covered with snow . . . through a cold and heavy rain we began descending one of the longest & steepest mountains yet passed over. But we got down it with safety. After reaching the bottom the scenery in the valley was the most rugged & sublime I ever beheld." He was describing the brilliantly-colored, desert-varnished cliffs of Navajo and Entrada sandstone, one of the first but far from the last to do so.

For the truly adventurous, a jeep trail of sorts winds down this gorge. But be warned: travel is risky here alone or without a winch and a short-wheelbase four-wheel drive vehicle.

From the bottom of the gorge, the trail continues down Hatch Wash to Highway 191, which it follows through beautiful, deeply eroded redrock country past Looking Glass Rock and Kane Springs into Spanish Valley. Pratt and his escort followed this valley, a classic example of a collapsed salt anticline, on to present-day Moab and the crossing of the Colorado.

Moab old-timers told Crampton the crossing was about half a mile downstream from the present highway bridge

just north of Moab. Pratt described the river as "about 350 yards wide & is the most rapid for its size I ever saw. It is dangerous to cross when high, & falls into a deep canion about 600 yards below the crossing." But they managed to swim men and horses across, and floated their goods across on a raft.

Still following Highway 191's present route, the trail ascended Courthouse Wash past deeply eroded red sandstone cliffs on the west and the arches and windows of what is today Arches National Park on the east. Topping out at Courthouse Spring, the trail angled off to the northwest through the barren, grey Mancos shale country of the Green River desert, relieved only by the great erosional Book and Roan Cliffs to the north, the distant Henry Mountains to the southwest. Travelers today can readily appreciate early-day complaints that in two days of hard riding to reach the Green River there was little grass and virtually no water.

The crossing of the Green was high adventure, at least to some. George Brewerton, traveling east with Kit Carson in 1848, described the building of a raft, which they launched with six men to pull it across:

" . . . we mismanaged the business altogether, until at length I fancy that the poor stream, already vexed beyond endurance, determined to take the matter under its own guidance . . . by abandoning us in disgust upon the same side from whence we had started, but more than a mile further down . . . Our situation was now far from pleasant, the only article of dress which we wore being our hats, the rest of our clothing having been left behind to come by another raft. To go up the rapids against the stream was out of the question, and

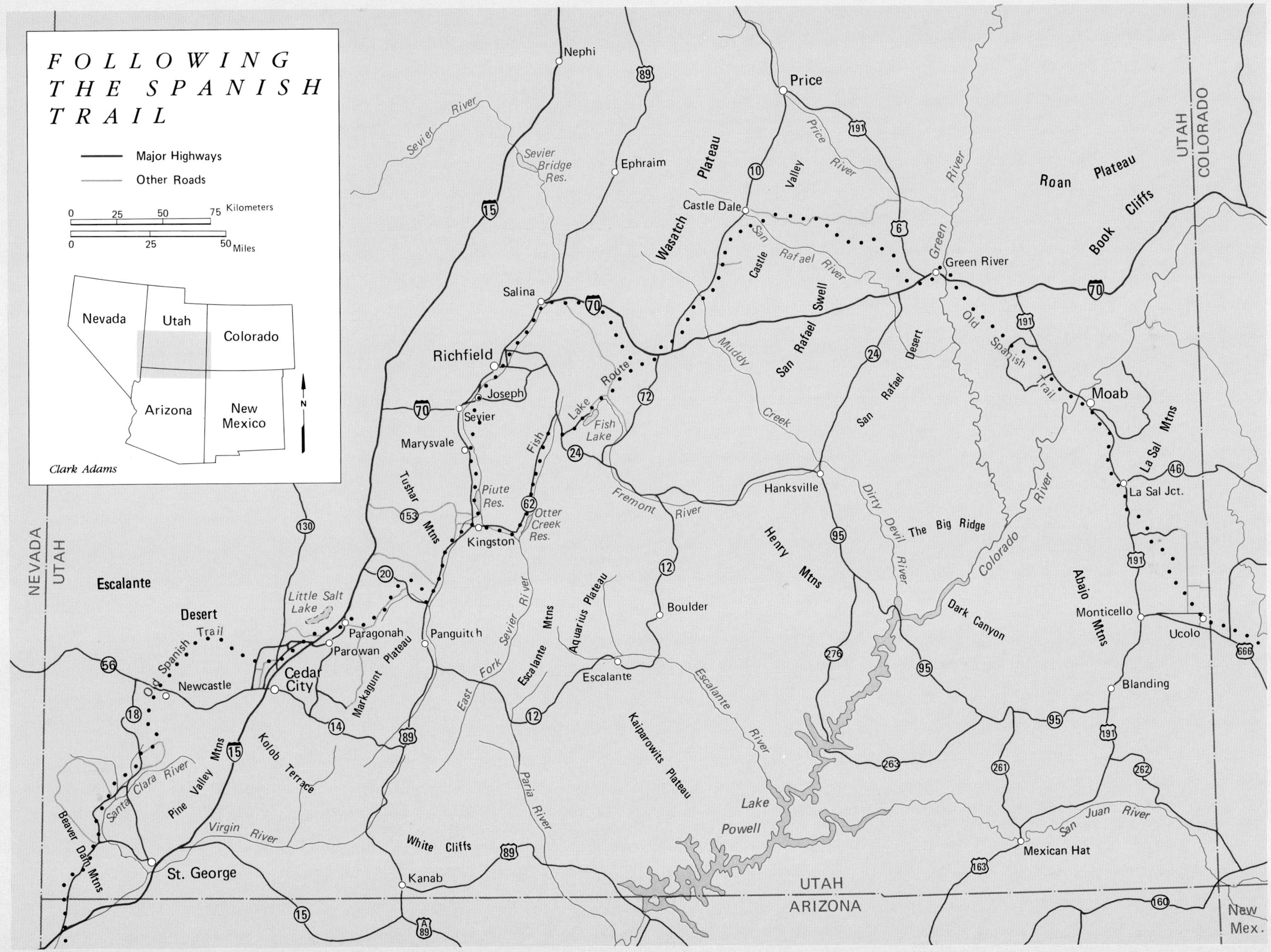

FOLLOWING THE SPANISH TRAIL

—— Major Highways
—— Other Roads

0   25   50   75 Kilometers

0   25   50 Miles

Nevada Utah Colorado

Arizona New Mexico

N

Clark Adams

NEVADA | UTAH

UTAH | COLORADO

UTAH
ARIZONA

New Mex.

Nephi
Price
Ephraim
Castle Dale
Wasatch Plateau
Roan Plateau
Book Cliffs
Salina
Green River
Richfield
Joseph
Sevier
Marysvale
San Rafael Swell
San Rafael Desert
Old Spanish Trail
Moab
La Sal Mtns
La Sal Jct.
Hanksville
Fish Lake
Piute Res.
Otter Creek Res.
Kingston
Tushar Mtns
Henry Mtns
The Big Ridge
Abajo Mtns
Monticello
Ucolo
Escalante
Desert
Little Salt Lake
Paragonah
Parowan
Panguitch
Aquarius Plateau
Boulder
Escalante
Blanding
Newcastle
Cedar City
Markagunt Plateau
Escalante Mtns
Kaiparowits Plateau
Dark Canyon
Kolob Terrace
Pine Valley Mtns
Virgin River
Lake Powell
Mexican Hat
Beaver Dam Mtns
Santa Clara River
White Cliffs
Kanab
San Juan River
St. George

Sevier River
Sevier Bridge Res.
Castle Valley
Price River
Green River
San Rafael River
Lake Route
Fish Lake
Fremont River
Muddy Creek
Dirty Devil River
Colorado River
Escalante River
Paria River
Old Spanish Trail

89 15 10 6 191 70 24 95 72 62 153 20 130 56 18 14 89 12 276 263 261 262 95 191 46 666 160 163 A 89

to cross from where we were, with a considerable fall and jagged rocks just below us, equally impossible. So we had no resource but to shoulder our baggage and travel back on foot . . . uttering more than one anathema upon the thorny plants, which wounded our unprotected feet at every step."

Their next attempt was more successful. Then it was the animals' turn:

"We selected a point upon our side considerably below . . . where the bank shelved gradually . . . Here we took our station to attract the attention of the swimming animals by shouting and whistling. Upon our signifying our readiness to receive them, one of the opposite party rode into the water upon the old bell-mare, and the frightened mules were forced to follow, urged on by the yells and blows of their drivers. In a few moments the whole caballada was under way; the old bell-mare, striking out and breasting the waves gallantly, while the mules, with only their heads and long ears visible above the water, came puffing like small high-pressure steam-boats in her wake. The yelling on our side now commenced, in which concert the Indians took the thorough base, performing to admiration; while our Mexican

muleteers rent the air with their favorite cry of 'anda mula,' 'hupar mula.' The animals, attracted by the noise, made straight for us and we soon had the gratification of seeing them safely landed, dripping and shaking themselves like so many Newfoundland dogs."

Kit Carson, as experienced a frontiersman as the west knew, lost "six rifles, three saddles, much ammunition, and nearly all our provisions" during the crossing. The Green was not to be taken lightly.

West from Green River, a modern four-wheeler can leave the highway and, with a good map, negotiate the trail through a series of rugged washes in the northern part of the San Rafael Swell, on through the Mancos Shale lowlands, across Buckhorn Wash and Buckhorn Flats, skirting south of heavily fossilized, 1000-foot-high cliffs of Cedar Mountain, and on into Castle Valley.

Lawyer Pratt didn't think too highly of this area in 1848. The country, he wrote, is "sandy, hilly & utterly barren. Water is also scarce, & if there is no mineral wealth in these mountains I can hardly conceive of what earthly use a large proportion of this

country was designed for!"

Things haven't changed much. A few abandoned uranium diggings dot the San Rafael Swell. An occasional stock watering tank serves winter-range cattle. Oil and gas and coal deposits attract developers in the cretaceous Book Cliffs and Cedar Mountain to the north and the Wasatch Plateau to the west. But the broad Mancos Shale lowlands are mostly left to the rabbit brush and greasewood and the rare dust plume of a lonely pickup.

It was not always so. An old railroad grade parallels and occasionally crosses the trail in this section. Cuts and fills are plainly visible, along with well-constructed stone culverts and bridge abutments. The work is mute evidence of abysmal planning. In 1882, the Denver and Rio Grande Railroad was seeking the best route from its railhead at Green River to Los Angeles. One proposal was a route that basically followed the Old Spanish Trail west through the San Rafael Swell to Buckhorn Flat and Castle Valley, then over the Wasatch Plateau to Salina to join a line running through Sevier Valley and on south to Los Angeles. The other route, eventually chosen, was to Provo

by way of Price and Spanish Fork Canyon.

Before the decision was final, D&RG had spent $217,000 grading fifty miles along the Spanish Trail route. The company paid Chinese workers $1.10 a day. Ruins of rock huts they built for shelter still stand near Chimney Rock in the San Rafael Swell. Tracks were never laid.

John Jorgensen grew up in the long-vanished town of Wilsonville, right on the Old Spanish Trail, and learned from his father where the trail went through Castle Valley. He and local historian Montell Seeley pointed out the one place where the old trail is clearly visible. From Red Seeps, a favorite waterhole at the base of Little Cedar Mountain, eight miles east of Castle Dale, it's plain to see where the trail climbed over low, rocky hills before dropping down to Huntington Creek. It's worth a short hike along the depression the trail left in the gravelly ridge.

Wide and level, Castle Valley is well-watered by Muddy, Ferron, Cottonwood, and Huntington creeks. There would be no need for horses to single-file through this region, and they didn't. Gunnison's party reported: "The Span-

ish Trail though seldom used of late years, is still very distinct where the soil washes but slightly. On some such spaces today we counted from fourteen to twenty parallel trails, of the ordinary size of Indian trails or horse paths, on a way barely fifty feet in width."

Local lore—and at least one guidebook—tells of an inscription on a cliff wall that, if genuine, would be of tremendous historical significance. With the help of a local resident, we found the wall, where Moore Road drops into Dry Wash at the south end of Castle Valley. The name of the early Spanish trader Arze and the date 1812 are written in brown paint. In the same brown paint are the names of Fremont and Gunnison and the date 1846; also some crude Indian pictographs. Giving the perpetrator credit for historical knowledge, it is plain from the sameness of the paint and the unlikely location, since there is no water or any conceivable camping place in the vicinity, that the inscriptions are fake.

Leaving Castle Valley, the main branch of the Old Spanish Trail crossed the Wasatch Plateau to the Sevier River, roughly along the present route of I-70

through Salina Canyon. At the mouth of Red Creek near Fremont Junction, the south branch split off for a short-cut over the 11,500-foot Fish Lake Mountains. In 1848, Brewerton, with Kit Carson, went that way and described Fish Lake in terms shivering modern campers can appreciate:

"... we encamped one evening upon a beautiful little lake situated in a hollow among the mountains, but at so great an elevation that it was, even in summer, surrounded by snow, and partially covered with ice ..."

But some things have changed: "... two of our men came into camp," *Brewerton continued,* "with as many fish as they could carry, and told us that they had caught as many more, but left them upon the banks of the lake. It seemed that in wandering about, they had discovered a little stream, a tributary to the lake, but quite shallow; this stream they represented as swarming with fish, so that they had gone in and killed them with sticks ... By sunrise the next morning we were ... up to our knees in the icy water ... such a slaughter of the finny tribe I have rarely seen. For my own part, with an old bayonet fastened to a stick, I caught five dozen—and a twinge of rheumatism ..."

From Fish Lake, this branch of the trail descends Otter Creek through lovely Grass Valley and rejoins the main trail on the Sevier River near Kingston. Travelers on the main trail, as they do today, found the Sevier Valley south from Salina to be delightful country.

"The valley of the Sevier, where we struck it, is the finest I have seen since leaving the United States," *Pratt wrote in 1848.* "Many thousand acres of the best of bottom land all lie in a body, and the surrounding hills will supply an ample quantity of stone coal. Deer, elk, mountain sheep, and all sorts of game incident to the mountains, are here found in great abundance."

Again, the next day: "Grass was fair and the water of the finest kind I ever saw. This valley of the Sevier is truly the loveliest spot, all things considered, my eyes ever looked upon! Some day or other, & that not distant, it will swarm with hundreds of our enterprising countrymen and be regarded, as in truth it is, the garden of the great basin : ..." *Residents of such peaceful farming communities as Sigurd, Elsinore, Joseph, Marysvale, and Circleville would not disagree.*

At present-day Joseph, the trail left the Sevier and ran up Long Valley east of present Highway 89, to avoid the rugged narrows around Marysvale. Passable dirt roads now roughly follow the old trail to rejoin Highway 89 just north of Piute Reservoir.

At present-day Orton, the trail left idyllic Sevier Valley and swung west up Bear Creek, over the Markagunt Plateau and down a steep, rugged slope to Little Salt Lake in Parowan Valley. Off-roaders who follow the jeep road along the trail between Cottonwood Mountain and Little Creek Peak will nod agreement with Pratt's description of travel "up the steepest of hills, then down places which it would seem almost impossible to descend. again in deep and precipitous canions: until at length suddenly broke upon us one of the finest and most extensive valleys I have seen in the whole western country!"

He had reached the north end of Cedar Valley. A few miles south, near Enoch, the trail leaves the present route of I-70 and strikes west through this table-flat valley, through the low Granite Mountains with their iron mines, and onto the vast, flat expanse of the Escalante Desert. For an off-roader, exploring the trail through the ledgy pinyon-juniper forest of Granite Mountain and out through the Escalante Desert is a rewarding experience, especially in the company of such a genial and knowlegeable historian as Gregory Crampton. But be warned: When wet, even perfectly level red-dirt roads in this region can bog down a four-wheel drive outfit.

At Newcastle, where prosperous farmers now fill long rows of storage sheds with potatoes destined to become chips, a dirt road follows the trail up Meadow Creek, past the ghost town site of Holt, over a low divide, and down Holt Creek into historic Mountain Meadows. As countless travelers had done before and others, including the large party murdered here in 1857, would do later, the Pratt party stopped to rest and recruit its animals. "There is fine & tender grass growing *[here]* to fatten a thousand head of horses or cattle," *Pratt wrote.*

Directly in front of the monument marking the Mountain Meadow massacre site runs the wash of Magotsu Creek. The old trail followed the lower part of this creek down to its junction with the Santa Clara below the massive volcanic Pine Valley Mountains. No jeep road descends this route; an eleven-mile hike from the pavement at Mountain Meadows to that at Veyo leads today's adventurer along the most primitive and rugged remaining section of the Old Spanish Trail.

From Shivwits south, the trail follows Jedediah Smith's 1827 trail along the present route of the county highway through the Paiute Indian Reservation and over Utah Hill, then down Beaver Dam Wash to the Virgin River below the narrows, and on to Las Vegas and eventually Los Angeles.

Through red rock canyons, over mountain passes, and across the long, dry valleys of the Great Basin, the Spanish Trail carved a 450-mile arc through Utah. The horse traders and thieves, the slavers and the vengeful Paiutes are long gone. But there are those places far from surfaced highways where on a still evening it's easy to imagine the clop of unshod hooves, the jingle of spurs, and the high-pitched cry of the muleteer, "Anda mula!"

Preceding pages left to right:
Ridges above the Spanish Valley
near Moab
Tom Till

La Sal Mountains and Moab
Valley through which the Spanish
Trail passed
Stephen Trimble

Little Grand Canyon of the San
Rafael River. The Spanish Trail
crossed the San Rafael upstream
from this gorge.
Scott T. Smith

Ranch near Circleville. Travel
along the Sevier River was the
most pleasant stretch of the
entire Spanish Trail
George Wuerthner

Left: Dell (or Redlum) Springs,
Skull Valley. This brackish,
almost undrinkable spring was
the last water before the eighty-
mile crossing of the Salt Desert.
John George

HASTINGS CUTOFF

If there is a freeway of historic trails in Utah, it is the thirty miles of Echo Canyon between the Wyoming line and Henefer. Down this easy grade came California-bound home-seekers, including the Donner Party in 1846. Brigham Young and his pioneer party followed the next year, and then, in the next two decades, tens of thousands of other Mormons with their wagons and handcarts. Echo Canyon was the overland passage to the California goldfields in 1849. In 1857, its rugged cliffs looked down on Johnston's Army, no longer invaders but reduced to entering the territory by Mormon permission. The Pony Express in 1860-61 kicked up Echo Canyon dust, as did virtually every overland emigrant to Utah or California from 1846 until the railroad ended the pioneer era in 1869. And even then, it was down this canyon that rail passengers rode.

Why? Because that's what the land dictates. In the arid west, trail-finders follow water; Indians had been trailing down Echo Canyon Creek for centuries. They find the easiest passage, and this valley was by far the best route for wagons through the Wasatch Mountains. It is no accident that the railroad and, much later, the main east-west freeway went that way.

So, this route was inevitable. But credit two men with hastening its use.

One was the indefatigable Mountain Man, Jedediah Smith, who in 1826 discovered, or rediscovered, South Pass. Following his trail, wagon trains could ascend the Sweetwater River and cross the Continental Divide on a grade so easy they hardly knew when they reached the 7550-foot summit. They would follow Smith's blaze down Little and Big Sandy creeks to the Green River, then Muddy Creek and Blacks Fork to Fort Bridger. From there, the Oregon Trail swung northwest to Fort Hall and the Snake River. By 1846, thousands of settlers had followed that trail to Oregon or had left it at Soda Springs to cut across the northwest corner of Utah to the Humboldt and the challenge of the Sierras to reach California.

The other man was Lansford Hastings. Out of California he rode with a dream to bring more Americans to the Pacific, end Spanish rule there, perhaps even be president himself of the new republic. To get settlers there quicker, he proposed a new route. Why make that long northern loop to Fort Hall? Why not save 250 miles by heading west from Fort Bridger, crossing the Wasatch by way of Echo Canyon, swinging around the south end of Great Salt Lake and then heading straight across the salt flats to Nevada and the Humboldt River?

In 1846, James Clyman, the veteran Mountain Man, guided Hastings on his ride east across the salt flats along a route John C. Fremont had taken the previous year. Twenty years earlier, Clyman had sailed a bull-boat around Great Salt Lake; he knew the Great Basin as few others did. Of the salt flats he wrote:

"This is the most desolate country perhaps on the whole globe, there being not one spear of vegetation and of course no kind of animal can subsist, and it is not yet ascertained to what extent this immense salt and sand plain can be south of where we are . . . " He argued strongly against the cutoff.

But Hastings was made of less practical stuff. Hurrying past the present-day site of Salt Lake City, through the Wasatch Mountains, and on past Fort Bridger, he met westward-bound emigrants with glowing reports of his new route.

There were some difficulties, he acknowledged, chiefly the forty-mile stretch without grass or water across the salt flats. But it was level and the going would be fast. Hadn't he just made the journey himself? Hadn't the great Fremont crossed only the previous year?

Unfortunately for the Donners, Hastings omitted a few details and was mistaken about others. He failed to point out that he as well as Fremont had traveled by mule and horseback, and that horse trails do not necessarily work as wagon roads. He underestimated the distance across the salt desert by half, calling it forty miles instead of eighty. He dreadfully miscalculated—if he calculated at all—the effort required to take wagons through the Wasatch Mountains and across the awful clay and mud of the salt desert.

Letters written by emigrants testify to the picture Hastings painted. One traveler wrote his brother back home: *"This route will cut off at least 250 miles, and is the one through which Capt. Fremont passed last season. It is proposed by Mr. Hastings; he . . . reports the route perfectly practicable for wagons.'*

Another emigrant added: *"The distance [from Ft. Bridger] to California was said to be six hundred and fifty miles, through a fine farming country, with plenty of grass for the cattle."* Anyone who has traveled I-80 across Utah's naked salt flats or across

Nevada's sage and greasewood deserts has to wonder what sort of farming Hastings could have had in mind.

Warned by James Clyman that the new route could be a death-trap, most of the emigrants that season chose to follow the known and well-traveled trail. But some listened to Hastings, and believed.

Among those who did were at least four parties with a total of seventy-seven wagons and about 250 people. A few others may have followed the new trail as well, but left no record.

First to take the Hastings Cutoff was a group of nine men mounted on mules and led by Edwin Bryant and William H. Russell. They bypassed Echo Canyon to the north, ascending Duck Creek from the vicinity of Evanston, then following Lost Creek down to the Weber River near Henefer. Rather than forcing their way down the Weber past the formidable obstacle of Devils Slide, they turned south up Main Canyon over Hogsback Ridge to East Canyon, then followed that creek through the narrows at the present-day damsite to the Weber and on down past Devils Gate to the valley. From his campsite at the mouth of Weber Canyon, Bryant noted a phenomenon that has changed little since then. Though he was ten miles away, he wrote, *"I could smell a strong and offensive fetor wafted from the shore of the lake."*

Bryant's excellent journal describes the ride into and through Salt Lake Valley, the Indians there, and their ways of catching, drying, and pulverizing grasshoppers. The party traded for a supply of ground grasshoppers mixed with crushed serviceberries, and Bryant noted, *"The prejudice against the grasshopper 'fruit-cake' was strong at first, but it soon wore off, and none of the delicacy was thrown away or lost."*

Thus fortified, the party rode to the vicinity of present-day Grantsville, through the Stansbury Mountains by way of steep, rugged North Willow Canyon, and camped at the springs in Skull Valley, where the Mormons would later establish the colony of Iosepa for Hawaiian converts. This was the last good water; there would be no more until they reached the foot of Pilot Peak, eighty miles away on what would become the Utah-Nevada state line. It took eighteen exhausting hours to cover those miles. But they did it with no loss of mules, and pushed on to reach Sutter's Fort on August 31, forty-two days from Fort Bridger.

But that was by muleback. Taking wagons over the trail was a different matter, as the next group would discover. This was a large party of forty wagons led by George Harlan and Samuel C. Young. Lansford Hastings himself was supposed to guide them, but, fortunately for them, he was somewhere on the trail behind. They found their own way through the Wasatch.

Believing that Weber Canyon was too rugged for wagons, Hastings intended that emigrants follow his trail south from Henefer into East Canyon and over Big Mountain to Salt Lake Valley. But the Harlan/Young party misunderstood or ignored this advice and hacked and swore their way down the Weber, fighting through the Wasatch in seven days rather than the sixteen it would take the Donners to follow Hastings' route. Roderic

Opposite left: Indian paintbrush, Stansbury Mountains. The Hastings Cutoff skirted the north end of these mountains.
John George

Opposite right: Prickly pear cactus along the Great Salt Lake shoreline north of the Hastings Cutoff
Tom Till

Korns' classic book, *West From Fort Bridger*, quotes a reminscence by W. W. Allen and R. B. Avery describing the ordeal:

"The canyon is scarcely wide enough to accomodate the narrow river which traverses it, and there was no room for roads between its waters and the abrupt banks. In many places great boulders had been rolled by the mountain torrents and lodged together, forming an impassable way . . . Three such obstacles were encountered, and only about a mile a day was averaged for more than a week. The sides of the mountains were covered by a dense growth of willows, never penetrated by white men. Three times spurs of the mountains had to be crossed by rigging the windlass on top, and lifting the wagons almost bodily. The banks were very steep, and covered with loose stones, so that a mountain sheep would have been troubled to keep its feet, much more an ox team drawing a heavily loaded wagon . . . While hoisting a yoke of oxen and a wagon up Weber mountain, the rope broke near the windlass. As many men as could surround the wagon were helping all they could by lifting at the wheels and sides. The footing was untenable and before the rope could be tied to anything, the men found they must abandon the wagon & oxen to destruction, or be dragged to death themselves. The faithful beasts seemed to comprehend their danger, and held their ground for a few seconds, and were then hurled over a precipice at least 75 feet high, and crushed in a tangled mass with the wagon on the rocks at the bottom of the canyon."

Whether this episode took place at Devils

Slide or lower down at Devils Gate or at some other treacherous spot is not known, but the account speaks eloquently of the character of Weber Canyon before it was blasted open to make way for a railroad and a freeway.

Next on the cutoff was a party of eight young men with four wagons. This group has been given the name of a young Swiss immigrant, Heinrich Lienhard, because of the colorful and detailed journal he wrote. They tackled the canyon differently. Spirited and free of family responsibilities, they simply drove their wagons down the river, getting through the worst part in one day. Lienhard described that day:

"On Aug. 6 we ventured upon this furious passage, up to this point decidedly the wildest we had encountered, if not the most dangerous. We devoted the entire forenoon and until fully one o'clock in the afternoon to the task of getting our four wagons through. In places we unhitched from the wagon all the oxen except the wheel-yoke, then we strained at both hind wheels, one drove, and the rest steadied the wagon; we then slid rapidly down into the foaming water, hitched the loose oxen again to the wagon and took it directly down the foaming riverbed, full of great boulders, on account of which the wagon quickly lurched from one side to the other; now we had to turn the wheels by the spokes, then again hold back with all the strength we had, lest it sweep upon a low lying rock and smash itself to pieces. In going back for each wagon we had to be very careful lest we lose our footing on the slippery rocks under the water

and ourselves be swept down the rapid, foaming torrent. When I began the journey, I had three pairs of boots and one pair of shoes. Today I was given the last service by the one remaining pair of boots . . . Henceforth I must manage to make my own footgear."

For those who still believe the myth that the Mormon pioneers found a barren desert when they arrived a year later, Lienhard's description of the valley of the Great Salt Lake Valley is instructive:

"The land extends from the mountains down to the lake in a splendid inclined plane broken only by the fresh water running down from ever-flowing springs above. The soil is a rich, deep black sand composition doubtless capable of producing good crops. The clear, sky-blue surface of the lake, the warm sunny air, the nearby high mountains, with the beautiful country at their foot, through which we on a fine road were passing, made on my spirits an extraordinary charming impression. The whole day long I felt like singing and whistling; had there been a single family of white men to be found living here, I believe that I would have remained. Oh, how unfortunate that this beautiful country was uininhabited!"

Generations of Utahns can identify with another description from this remarkable journal. After telling of a swim in Great Salt Lake, marveling at the clear water and its buoyancy, he concluded:

"Only a single feature had the swimming in this lake that was not conducive to pleasure; this consisted in the fact that when one got a little water in one's eye, it occasioned

Opposite above: Desert Peak in the Newfoundland Mountains. Hastings' trail, now inundated by the West Desert Pond, crossed the Salt Flats through the north end of the Silver Island Mountains, right background.
Rick Reese

Opposite below: Archaeologists excavate mounds where the Donner-Reed wagons were abandoned in the Salt Flats in 1846. The West Desert pumping project subsequently flooded this site.
Tom Smart

a severe burning pain; and after we reached the shore and dressed ourselves without first washing in unsalted water, being desirous of hastening on, we soon experienced an almost unbearable smarting or itching over the whole body where the salt water had filled up all the crevices of the skin with an all-enveloping deposit of salt."

From the lake, the Harlan-Young and then the Lienhard companies followed the Bryant-Russell route to the beautiful springs at Grantsville, then around the north end of the Stansbury Mountains to the springs at Iosepa before attacking the eighty miles of salt desert and mud flats that lay between them and the next good water at Pilot Springs.

For the Harlan-Young party, the ordeal of taking the first wagons across the salt flats was sheer horror. Three days and nights it took, and the lives of unrecorded numbers of oxen. Wagons were abandoned as far as thirty miles short of Pilot Springs, and they spent days retracing their steps to recover them, once water was reached. But they managed to regroup, and moved on to California, reaching it two weeks later than if they had stayed on the Fort Hall trail.

Lienhard and his friends managed better. They made the desert crossing in two-and-a-half days of almost continuous driving and may have been the only party to cross those eighty deadly miles without losing a single ox.

Lienhard's subsequent career is particularly interesting. He became superintendent at Sutter's Fort and was there when men of the Mormon Battalion were involved in the discovery of gold. He returned to Switzerland where he married and settled until 1856, when he found his way to Nauvoo, Illinois. There he bought the home Heber C. Kimball had abandoned when the Mormons fled in 1846; he lived in it until his death in 1903. It is one of history's strange twists that this young man who so wished he could settle in Salt Lake Valley lived for half a century in a Nauvoo Mormon home and preserved it so well it became the beginning and centerpiece of the Nauvoo restoration project.

Close behind the Harlan-Young and Lienhard wagon trains on the Hastings Cutoff came the Donner-Reed party, and the stage was set for tragedy. Their ordeal of starvation and cannibalism in the Sierras is remembered long after the names of successful parties are forgotten.

The *"ifs"* of history are nowhere more tantalizing than in the experiences of the Donners. If they had not listened to Hastings and taken his cutoff in the first place . . . If they had cooperated and worked together . . . If many of their oxen had not run off and been lost in the desert . . . If stalwart James Reed had not lost his head and killed James Snyder at a Nevada stream crossing and been banished from the party . . . If the Digger Indians along the Humboldt River had not avenged past atrocities by killing and running off the party's cattle . . . If snow had not come early to the Sierras that year and piled the deepest in memory . . . If any of this had been different, there might never have been that horror from which only forty-seven of the snow- trapped emigrants survived, many of them by eating the bodies of those who did not.

All these *"ifs"* have been well argued by historians. Less discussed are some of the decisions made during the crossing of the Wasatch. One involves the steep, short hill at the mouth of Emigration Canyon, where luxury condominiums now sit, and where the Donner Party made a fatal mistake. But before examining those decisions, we need to know who these Donners and their associates were. How did they come to this place? Why were they the first to take wagons down Emigration Canyon?

George and Jacob Donner were brothers from Springfield, Illinois. With them were their wives and twelve children. The company's leader for most of the way was James Frazier Reed, also from Springfield; he brought his wife and four children. Others from Illinois included Franklin Ward Graves, his wife and nine children, and William H. Eddy, his wife and two children. The Patrick Breens and their seven children came from Keokuk, Iowa; the Murphy and Pike families, twelve persons in all, from Jackson County, Missouri. From Germany came Lewis Keseberg, his wife and two children, and a Mr. and Mrs. Wolfinger. Including various single men, mostly teamsters, there were eighty-seven people in the party, ranging from babes in arms to a woman of seventy. Some were well-to-do, some poor. A few had experience on the frontier; most did not. They had come together partly by design, partly by the chance of the trail.

Persuaded by Hastings, they left the Fort Hall road at Fort Bridger on July 31 and followed the tracks of the earlier wagons. Making good time, they cut down across the Big

Muddy and Bear rivers, into the open bottoms of Echo Canyon and finally to the Weber where it begins its plunge through the Wasatch. There, at the site of present-day Henefer, they made their second wrong decision. The Harlan-Young and Lienhard wagons had already forced their way through the canyon, but Hastings had other ideas. He and James Clyman had traced a trail up Parleys Canyon, over Big Mountain, and down East Canyon, and that was the way he wanted the wagons to go. So he rode back a couple of miles and left a note for the emigrants in a clump of sagebrush. Weber Canyon was too rough and dangerous, he wrote. If they would send a messenger after him, he would return and show them a shorter and better route.

The note was found, and the messengers were sent—Reed, Pike, and a single man, Charles Stanton. The three rode some eighty-five miles in two days, nearly killing their horses, and overtook Hastings at the south end of Great Salt Lake. On a borrowed horse, Reed returned with Hastings to the top of Big Mountain, where Hastings pointed out the *"shorter, safer route"* and then turned back toward California. The company remained in camp four precious days waiting Reed's return.

The new route proved neither shorter nor safer. It was, in fact, a sixteen-day ordeal of laboring up summit after weary summit, pitching and bouncing along miles of treacherous sidehills, crossing and recrossing brush-choked streams, hacking and digging through willows, brush, timber and rocks until hands bled and tempers grew short.

Before it ended, the first ugly signs of disunity and character weakness appeared; James Reed reported the men would not work a quarter of the time. And every member of the party who could read a calendar or recognize the signs of the season knew they were in peril.

Sixteen days to cover thirty-six miles. Nowhere else on the journey did they encounter such delays. Not in the glue-like mud of the salt flats. Not along the Humboldt, even after Indians had run off or killed more than two dozen of their oxen, leaving the remainder barely able to pull. Not even the struggle up the east slopes of the Sierras, before the snow. Reed later argued that it was not the delays in the Wasatch that doomed the party; history does not agree.

There is little written record of those sixteen days. Reed's journal gives the barest outline—a few words a day. But the land is still there, much of it changed little in more than a century. The Mormon pioneers followed the Donner footsteps a year later, and the trail can be traced foot by foot through their journals.

Much of the trail can be traveled on paved highway. Those willing to walk can find choice sections of the trail very nearly as they were in pioneer days. Stone monuments erected by Explorer Scouts under my direction in the late 1950s mark points of interest, though vandals have destroyed or carried off most of the bronze plaques. Even so, residents along the Wasatch Front can find no more convenient and rewarding way to relive history than by driving or, especially, hiking over this trail.

After four days of waiting for Reed to return, the wagon train got under way. Six miles after heading south up Main Canyon along the route of present-day Highway 65, they crossed Hogsback Ridge and got their first good look at what they faced. William Clayton, with the Mormon pioneers a year later, noted at this spot that *"The country west looks rough and mountainous"*; it must have looked equally forbidding to the Donners.

Fifty yards short of the Hogsback summit, to the right of the present road, parallel ruts show where the Donner wagon wheels and the thousands to follow ground deep into the solid rock.

The present road drops from the Hogsback down Dixie Hollow to East Canyon Creek. The Donners tried that route, but found it far too brushy. Instead, they turned west and made their way over difficult sidehills to East Canyon Creek about half a mile above the present dam. Then came three days of hard labor to cut a way up this beautiful stream. Orson Pratt's 1847 pioneer journal describes the effort:

"We followed the dimly traced wagon tracks up this stream for 8 miles, crossing the same 13 times. The bottoms of this creek are thickly covered with willows, from 5 to 15 rods wide, making an immense labor in cutting a road through for the emigrants last season. We still found the road almost impassable, and requiring much labor."

The first couple of miles of this trail are now drowned in the waters of East Canyon Reservoir. Three miles south of the head of the reservoir, the paved highway swings to

ten to the base by means of ropes held hard by the men . . . Some of the heavier wagons got to dragging pretty rapidly, and one at least went down with a rush, oversetting at the foot of the descent, a wreck and a ruin—tongue, wheels, mess-chests, camp-kettles and all. This being a Dragoon wagon, the Infantry boys laughed—which proceeding the Dragoons regarded as unfitting and disrespectful . . . We found, going down, such clouds and density of dust as well nigh brought us to open suffocation."

The path of that descent is plain to see. Thousands of wheels left ruts that have since eroded into a sizable gully that runs straight down the mountainside, crossing the present-day switchbacking highway at several points. Hikers can follow the trail to the bottom and on down to Mountain Dell Fork near the Birch Springs campground.

From here, the trail followed an easy grade through a fairly wide valley, much of it to be covered by the waters of Little Dell reservoir. It is almost accidental that the Donners didn't continue on down Parleys Canyon. In Little Dell, they met Pike and Stanton, who days before had ridden with Reed to overtake Hastings. After resting their horses, the two men had backtracked and made their way up Parleys Canyon. Parleys was too rough for wagons, they reported.

So, in what may have been their third wrong decision, they turned west and climbed the deceptively steep 1.5-mile east slope of Little Mountain. The route is still clearly visible; erosion in the old wheel ruts has left a gully running right to the pass where the highway now crosses. Equally

clear is the route down the other side to Emigration Creek, 4.5 miles above the canyon mouth.

Cutting through the dense brush and clearing the boulders of those 4.5 miles took the weary travelers almost three more precious days. Nineteen times they had to cross the creek in that short distance.

Then, when they were almost out of these accursed Wasatch Mountains, they were stopped. The canyon walls narrowed, boulders choked the streambed, the brush seemed impenetrable. And they were bone-weary of that infernal chopping and digging.

Three times before—at Fort Bridger, at the entrance to Weber Canyon, in Mountain Dell—the party had turned away from the difficult to push into what seemed to be the easier unknown. Each time they got into deeper trouble. At the mouth of Emigration Canyon, they did it again. Rather than tackling that last narrow gorge, they chose to climb the short, steep hill at the south of the canyon's mouth. Condominium builders have cut away the top of Donner Hill, but from the bottom the magnitude of the emigrants' task is still obvious.

Virginia Reed, then twelve years old, later recalled that day: *"We reached the end of the canyon where it looked as though our wagons would have to be abandoned. It seemed impossible for the oxen to pull them up the steep hill and the bluffs beyond, but we doubled teams and the work was, at last, accomplished, almost every yoke in the train [of 23 wagons] being required to pull up each wagon."*

What this effort meant to the party's future

can only be guessed. Was their exhaustion from laboring up and down that hill twenty-three times the reason the oxen failed so badly on the salt flats? Certainly, the Donner party fared worse there than anyone else did—and no one else had suffered the ordeal of Donner Hill.

The tragedy of this final bad decision was made evident by the Mormons who came the next year. Following the Donner tracks all the way from the Weber—and profiting greatly by the previous year's labor on the road—they reached Donner Hill, and faced the same dilemma. William Clayton reported their decision:

"We found the road crossing the creek again to the south side and then ascending up a very steep, high hill. It is so very steep as to be almost impossible for heavy wagons to ascend and so narrow that the least accident might precipitate a wagon down a bank three or four hundred feet—in which case it would certainly be dashed to pieces. Colonel Markham and another man went over the hill and returned up the canyon to see if a road cannot be cut through and avoid this hill . . . Brother Markham says a good road can soon be made through the bushes some ten or fifteen rods. A number of men went to work immediately to make the road . . . After spending about four hours' labor the brethren succeeded in cutting a pretty good road along the creek and the wagons proceeded on."

Ten or fifteen rods—some 200 feet. A little foresight to scout out the trail. Four hours of willing, cooperative labor. Would this, for the Donner party, be the difference between life and death?

After this ordeal, the oxen needed rest. But there was no time. It was August 22, and the Sierras were still 500 miles away. So on they pushed, camping on the Jordan River [at about 27th South] the first night, near present-day Garfield the next, at Grantsville the third. Here, the consumptive Luke Halloran died and was buried beside John Hargrave, a member of the Harlan-Young party who had died a few days before. Theirs are the first recorded graves of white emigrants in Utah.

Still following the Harlan-Young tracks, the party skirted the Stansbury Mountains to the north and reached the last water, at Iosepa, in two days. They spent another day resting their livestock, gathering grass, and filling every container with water for the eighty-mile ordeal ahead. By this time, they must have realized how dreadfully wrong Hastings had been. And the worst was yet to come.

Certainly we questioned Hastings' judgment—if not his sanity—as we retraced the tracks of the Donner party across the salt flats a quarter-century ago. In just-developed wide-track vehicles, we joined a group of University of Utah historians and archaeologists in 1962 for what may have been the first complete crossing of the salt flats on the Donner trail in more than a century.

Northwest across Skull Valley the trail went, then through a low pass—Hastings Pass—in the Cedar Mountains. Where the trail crosses I-80, they were in the salt desert, with sixty miles to go to water.

It took the Donner-Reed party four days and nights of arduous labor to travel those sixty miles. Then there were seven more days of resting from the ordeal, hauling out mired wagons, and rounding up what cattle they could find, before they could move on toward California.

Following their trace, it was easy to see why. On the first part, approaching and leaving the long, low line of hills known as the Greyback, the trail wandered through head-high sand dunes, where dense clouds of dust nearly suffocated the emigrants. Hardly an encouraging approach to the more terrible ordeal that lay ahead.

Beyond the sand dunes stretch the salt flats, immense wastes of sandy, salty clay covered with a thin, glistening layer of salt crystals. They are perfectly level and look hard; surely a wagon could cross quickly, perhaps in a day and a night.

But under the thin crust, the clay was wet and sticky. The narrow wheels of the emigrant wagons sank deeply into it. So did the hooves of the oxen, the mud sticking in great gobs. It took enormous effort to pull loaded wagons through that muck—and forty miles of it lay ahead.

By the time the party had slogged to within three or four miles of Floating Island, loads were being dropped, wagons abandoned. From there it became a grim battle for survival as teams were cut loose from mired wagons and driven west toward Pilot Peak and the promised water more than twenty miles away.

Out of the mud they slogged at last and onto a low, rocky pass between Silver Island and Crater Island, two fantastically stark and rugged outcroppings. Here was relief at last; a few stunted sage and greasewood bushes seemed to testify that the lifeless flats were behind. There's a small spring under a ledge here, but they did not find it. No matter. They pressed on, believing that Pilot Springs was just ahead.

But as they topped the low pass, they gazed with horror at ten more miles of mud flats stretching between them and water. With men and animals near exhaustion and with the spring-fed willows in plain sight but so desperately far away across flats, crossing those ten miles must have been sheer agony.

Emigrants and animals slogged twenty-eight miles to water beyond the area where many could pull wagons no farther. Some wagons were recovered by teams backtracking from Pilot Springs; five were left forever in the desert. There is no record of how many animals were lost; one survivor put it at thirty-six. James Reed entered the desert with nine yoke of oxen, two to a yoke. He left it with one ox and a cow. *"Losing nine yoke of cattle here,"* he later wrote, *"was the first of my sad misfortunes."*

Our expedition in 1962 saw evidence of all that. Long, thin parallel lines stretched across the table-flat wastes. Wagon wheels long since rotted had churned up those tracks. The salt had glazed them to a perfect smoothness, and they remained mute witnesses to tragedy. There were more witnesses. East of Floating Island, a series of mounds marked, for some oxen and some wagons, the end of the struggle. A small mound held a jawbone and a few other bone fragments, marking where an ox had collapsed and died in its yoke. In a larger

Wind-blown sun flowers in Utah's West Desert country
John George

mound were a rotted wheel rim, a spoke or two, bits of harness, a salt-encrusted silver spoon, a corroded round object that could be a child's locket or a rouge box. So it went, mound after mound, the pitiful remnants of a party that barely escaped from the desert with its lives, only to suffer slow starvation and the horror of cannibalism in the Sierra Nevada snows.

I revisited the site in the fall of 1986 when archaeologists were carefully excavating the sites. They found little. In recent years, anyone with an ATV could reach the site, and looters had dug into the mounds and carried off anything they could find. The tracks were still there under the salt glaze, though, and with care would have remained for another century. But even that remnant of history is now gone. The project to pump water into the west desert to control the depth of Great Salt Lake has flooded the area, and all traces of the struggle through the salt desert have vanished.

Something else has vanished as well. In 1962, Pete McKellar and his wife lived and ranched alone at Pilot Springs, their clapboard house overlooking the last ten miles of the Donner-Reed party's desperate struggle. Tall willow trees arched over the quiet, shining pool that had witnessed the bawling of cattle and the human sobs of gratitude as they found life in these waters. A man could stand at Pilot Springs and hear echoes.

No more. Miles of barbed wire fence and no-trespassing signs now guard the orchards and grainfields a Texas-based agri-business has established here. Huge sheds shelter farm machinery and the semi-trailers and tractor trucks that roll the produce to market. Miles of pipes and sprinkler systems water the land. And the spring that meant so much? Sucked nearly dry by the wells that feed the sprinklers, it lies weed-grown, stinking, forgotten.

Epilogue. The Donner-Reed and Mormon experiences in the West are closely intertwined. Not only did the Mormons benefit greatly from the roadwork done on the Hastings Cutoff in 1846, but they also had a hand in the sad events at the California end of the trail. Through his newspaper in San Francisco, prominent Mormon Samuel Brannan helped organize efforts to rescue Donner-Reed survivors from the Sierras. Two Mormons were among the seven-man first relief party. Several members of the Mormon Battalion were with the bodyguard of General Stephen Kearney, who was taking John C. Fremont east to stand trial on charges of mutiny. When they came on the scene of death and cannibalism in the Sierras in spring of 1847, those men were detailed to bury the remains.

News of the Donner tragedy circulated among westering emigrants, but did not entirely dissuade travel over the salt desert. Gold fever lured some 500 people over that route in 1850, though few with wagons. The route was abandoned in the early 1850s after Howard Egan, J. H. Simpson and others marked out a longer but easier and safer road that skirted the salt desert to the south. The new road became the route of the Pony Express, the Overland Stage, and the Lincoln Highway. The salt flats were left to wind, sun, and memories.

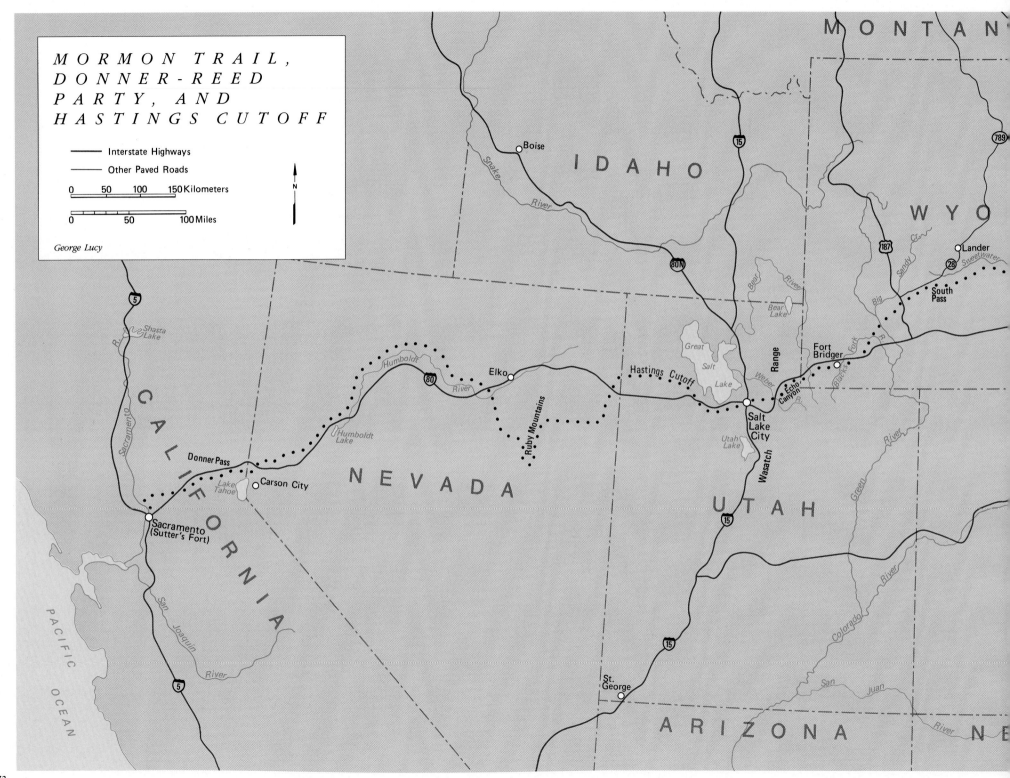

Interstate Highways
Other Paved Roads

0   50   100   150 Kilometers

0   50   100 Miles

N

George Lucy

MONTANA

IDAHO

WYO

Boise

80N

Snake River

Bear River

Bear Lake

Lander

789

187

Sweetwater

28

South Pass

5

Shasta Lake

CALIFORNIA

Sacramento River

Humboldt

Humboldt River

80

Elko

Great Salt Lake

Hastings Cutoff

Range

Fort Bridger

Weber

Big Sandy

Blacks Fork

Echo Canyon

Humboldt Lake

Ruby Mountains

Salt Lake City

Donner Pass

NEVADA

Lake Tahoe

Carson City

Utah Lake

Wasatch

UTAH

15

Green River

PACIFIC OCEAN

San Joaquin River

5

15

St. George

Colorado River

San Juan River

ARIZONA

NE

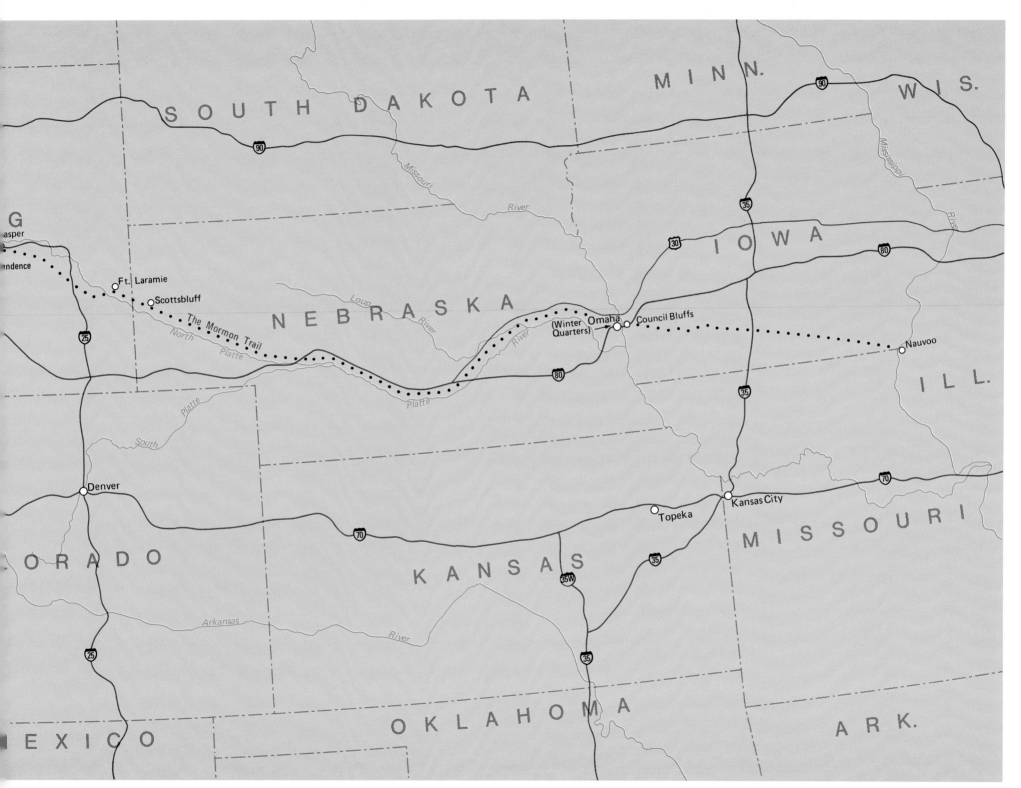

SOUTH DAKOTA

MINN.

WIS.

90

G

asper

endence

Ft. Laramie

Scottsbluff

The Mormon Trail

NEBRASKA

Loup

River

North

Platte

Platte

Platte

South

35

IOWA

30

80

(Winter
Quarters)

Omaha

Council Bluffs

80

Nauvoo

35

ILL.

Missouri

River

Mississippi

River

Denver

Kansas City

Topeka

MISSOURI

70

70

ORADO

KANSAS

35W

35

25

EXICO

OKLAHOMA

ARK.

35

Arkansas

River

25

Autumn in East Canyon. The Mormon pioneers had great difficulty cutting through the willows and brush here before climbing over Big Mountain.
John George

MORMON TRAIL

Rolling along the tracks laid down by the Donner-Reed party from Fort Bridger the previous year, Brigham Young's Mormon Pioneer Company found its way into the valley of the Great Salt Lake. It was the first trickle of what would be an astonishing flood. During the next twenty years, The Gathering to Zion brought more than 68,000 other Mormons over the trail, swallowing the dust of 9,600 wagons or toiling at the shafts of 650 handcarts to reach their Promised Land. Of those who started the 1,200-mile odyssey, 6,000 pioneers ended it in unmarked graves along the way.

The Mormons made no new trail. For 600 miles through Nebraska to Fort Laramie, they kept to the north side of the Platte River rather than risk conflicts with wagon trains on the more heavily traveled south side. But that route was not new; the Oregon Trail ran on both sides of the river. Crossing the Platte to the south side at Fort Laramie, the Mormons stayed on the Oregon Trail over South Pass, cut down to Fort Bridger on the California Trail, then followed the Donner-Reed tracks to Salt Lake Valley.

But if they were not trail blazers, the Mormons were road builders. They were different than any seen before or since on west-bound trails. Instead of hurrying through the country as others had done, they were coming to stay. Their road-building was not just to get their own wagons through; it would serve the thousands of others they knew would follow.

They moved with discipline and purpose unknown among any other westering people. Every ax stroke, every pick-and-ple. Every ax stroke, every pick-and-

shoveling aside of every rock was part of The Gathering. The road they were building was to be the trunk from which branches would spread out to establish and colonize a 1,000-mile inland empire.

Quickly, that became apparent. During the first week after the Pioneer Company reached the valley, while many were damming streams, flooding the land, and planting crops, others fanned out to explore the country, south to Utah Lake, north to Ogden and Cache Valleys. Before a month was out, two wagon trains, one of them carrying Brigham Young, were on the trail back to Winter Quarters to organize more companies to come the following year.

On the way, they met what became known as the Big, or First, Company, led by Brigham's brother, John, and including such leaders as John Taylor, Parley P. Pratt, Charles C. Rich, and Eliza R. Snow. With 566 wagons, some 2,000 people and 5,000 head of livestock, it was by far the largest company yet seen anywhere on the plains and the first to be organized in the unique Mormon system of companies of tens, fifties, and hundreds. This throng reached the valley in early October, in time to suffer through a cold, hungry winter. Thousands more came the following year.

In a way no other western trail did, the Mormon Trail became a two-way highway. For twenty years, until rails down Echo Canyon ended the pioneer era, that road carried a steady inward flow of gathering Mormons but also a steady outward flow of teams and wagons to bring supplies and to assist new emigrants into the valley. It also

carried missionaries heading to the eastern United States and Europe to help swell the flood of new converts. How well they succeeded: Of the 68,000 Mormons who trudged the trail during those twenty years, some 47,000 were converts from Britain, Scandinavia, and Germany.

So, though the first tracks were not theirs, this was, in every sense but its discovery, the Mormon Trail.

The journey that brought the first Mormons into the valley on July 21, 1847, and Brigham Young three days later, had begun twenty-four years earlier when fourteen-year-old Joseph Smith received the first of a series of visions that were to put an entire people on the march. From its birthplace in upstate New York, the infant but growing church Smith organized made its way to Kirtland, Ohio [now a suburb of Cleveland]. Bankruptcy and criminal charges after some disastrous banking efforts drove Joseph and his flock from there to western Missouri. From there, bitter, bloody opposition by the old settlers drove them out again—this time into Illinois to build a new city, Nauvoo, on the banks of the Mississippi.

But there was no peace. As the church grew, so did opposition to it. By the winter and early spring of 1845-1846, mourning their murdered prophet and driven by armed mobs from their Nauvoo homes, the Mormons were struggling across Iowa to establish Winter Quarters on the west bank of the Missouri and to prepare for the long trek west.

Mormon poetess Eliza R. Snow wrote a woman's view of that bitter beginning:

Autumn leaves, East Canyon Creek
Pete Houdeshel

" . . . on the first night of the encampment, nine children were born into the world, and from that time on, as we journeyed onward, mothers gave birth to offspring under almost every variety of circumstances imaginable; some in tents, others in wagons; in rainstorms and snowstorms.

" . . . one birth occurred under the rude shelter of a hut with a bark roof, the sides of which were formed of blankets fastened to poles stuck in the ground, through which the rain was dripping. Kind sisters stood holding dishes to catch the water as it fell, thus protecting the newcomer and its mother as the little innocent first entered on the stage of human life . . .

"Let it be remembered that [most of] *the mothers of these wilderness-born babies were . . . born and educated in the eastern states, had there embraced the gospel and for the sake of their religion had gathered with the saints and under trying circumstances had assisted with their faith, patience, and energies in making Nauvoo what its name indicates—-'The Beautiful.' "*

Out of Iowa's frozen mud during those early days of disorganized exodus came William Clayton's hymn of The Gathering—"Come, Come, Ye Saints." I thought about that on a bitter cold morning in March 1978 while running the first ten-mile leg of a *Deseret News*-sponsored relay from Nauvoo to Salt Lake City. As I panted up the bluffs above the Mississippi, I tried to imagine 2,000 Saints in their skiffs and barges dodging ice floes as they fled across the river from Nauvoo. Running past Sugar Creek, I remembered that temperatures in February 1846 had dropped as low as twelve below zero in the camp there, freezing a mile-wide bridge across the river. Running through rolling farm country beyond, I thought of the ordeal they faced in that struggle across Iowa, and of the dreadful winter ahead on the west bank of the Missouri. With all that, Clayton's words came home: *" . . . And should we die before our journey's through, all is well; all is well."*

By early April 1847, when Brigham Young was ready to start the Pioneer Company west from the tents and dugouts of Winter Quarters, 600 graves marked where for that many Saints the journey was through. The fear of adding another grave was one reason Brigham's neatly ordered Pioneer Company of 144 men—twelve men for each of the twelve tribes of Israel—did not stay that way. Harriet Young, the wife of Brigham's younger brother, Lorenzo Dow Young, suffered from asthma; she would die, too, she protested, if left behind. Because Lorenzo declared he wouldn't go without her, Brigham reluctantly agreed to take her. But Harriet couldn't be the only woman, so Brigham decided that his wife, Clara, Harriet's daughter by a previous marriage, could go along as well. Once that was decided, it was no big thing to add Heber C. Kimball's wife, Ellen, to the company's rolls. By the time Harriet also insisted on bringing her two younger children, Brigham must have been too weary to argue.

So they started, April 5, 1847—144 men, three women, two young boys. With experience gained in the Iowa crossing, and under Brigham's sometimes-wrathful discipline, the Pioneer Company was as successful as any ever seen on the trail. Improving the road where necessary and leaving men behind to build ferries and assist later companies, the company reached Salt Lake Valley in 111 days, with no deaths and no serious accidents.

But it didn't come easily or without contention or without the tongue-lashings for which Brigham became justly famous. These were imperfect humans, who required considerable refining to qualify for what Brigham had in mind. One memorable scolding, May 29 on the Platte River near Chimney Rock, illustrates the point:

"When I wake up in the morning, the first thing I hear is some of the brethren jawing each other and quarreling because a horse has got loose in the night. I have let the brethren dance and fiddle . . . night after night to see what they will do . . . Well, they will play cards, they will play checkers, they will play dominoes, and if they had the privilege and were where they could get whiskey, they would be drunk half their time, and in one week they would quarrel, get to high words and draw their knives and kill each other."

He expected more of men who held the priesthood, he scolded. *"Do you suppose that we are going to look out a home for the Saints, a resting place, a place of peace where they can build up the kingdom and bid the nations welcome, with a low, mean, dirty, trifling, covetous, wicked spirit dwelling in our bosoms?"*

Cleansed of any such spirit, the wagons moved on, William Clayton counting each time a rag tied to a wheelspoke of Heber Kimball's wagon touched the ground. The wheel measured 14' 8" in circumference, and rolled along at 360 revolutions per mile. From that calculation, he and Orson Pratt designed a roadometer, which Appleton Harmon whittled out of wood. With its help, Clayton placed the first accurate mileage markers along the trail.

Hunting buffalo and antelope, finding dinosaur bones, killing—and being bitten by—rattlesnakes, relieved the dusty tedium of the trail through western Nebraska and into Wyoming. On June 1, the party reached Fort Laramie, where they were met by a group of Saints from Mississippi who had reached Fort Laramie the previous year and had spent the winter at Pueblo waiting for Brigham's arrival. Soon to arrive, also, were members of the Sick Detachment who had dropped out of the Mormon Battalion's long march to California and had also spent the winter at Pueblo. The two groups, 275 Mormons in all, would travel with or close behind the Pioneer Company the rest of the way to Salt Lake Valley.

West of Fort Laramie, bluffs crowding close to the river forced the Mormons to leave their trail north of the Platte and follow the more heavily traveled trail on the south side. That meant jockeying with other wagon trains for campsites and good grass. The trail was crowded in 1847; one group of packers told the Mormons at Fort Laramie that they had counted no less than 2,000 wagons on the trail between there and Missouri.

Many of the travelers were Missourians.

Remembering the violence and murders that had driven the Mormons from that state, the two groups viewed each other with apprehension. But there were no conflicts. In fact, with the Platte River in flood stage, the Mormons used their leather boat, the *"Revenue Cutter,"* to ferry the Missourians' goods across. It took twenty-four crossings at $1.50 a load.

The Missourians paid their bill with 1300 pounds of flour and some corn meal and bacon, which, William Clayton noted, came as *"a great blessing inasmuch as a number of the brethren have had no breadstuff for some days."* Wilford Woodruff put it in more Biblical terms: *"It looked as much a miracle to see our supplies replenished in the midst of the black hills as it did to have the children of Israel fed with manna in the wilderness."*

After that profitable bit of business and after struggling for five exhausting days to get their own wagons across the river, Brigham saw some interesting possibilities. He put the Mormons to work building a ferry and left nine of the pioneers behind to operate it. For years, the Mormon ferry at what would become Casper, Wyoming profited by carrying emigrants across the Platte.

Moving up the Platte to its confluence with the Sweetwater and just beyond, the company reached the great granitic dome of Independence Rock. Wilford Woodruff and John Brown climbed it and found names—still visible today—carved by trappers, emigrants, and others as early as 1812. Characteristically, the Mormons improved the occasion by kneeling in prayer for the wel-

fare of the Pioneer Company and their wives and families.

Following the Sweetwater, the train pushed on without incident to South Pass, which they crossed on June 27, a Sunday. It was three years to the day since Joseph Smith had been murdered in his jail cell in Carthage, Illinois.

"Our minds have reverted back to the scenes at Carthage jail," William Clayton wrote, *"and it is a gratification that we have so far prospered in our endeavors to get from under the grasp of our enemies."* Clayton noted *"the satisfaction of seeing the current run west instead of east,"* but missing in the written record is any sense of symbolism. In crossing the Continental Divide that day, the Mormons were crossing their own divide, from mobocracy and fear in the east to sanctuary and peace in the west.

They were soon to get plenty of advice about that sanctuary. At Pacific Springs, just over South Pass, Moses Harris, veteran of twenty-five years of trapping in the mountains, offered his services as a guide. His report of the country ahead was not encouraging.

"From his description, we have little chance to hope for even a moderately good country anywhere in those regions," William Clayton recorded. *"He speaks of the whole region as being destitute of timber and vegetation, except the wild sage."*

Despite Clayton's observation that Harris *"appears to be a man of intelligence,"* his services were declined; the pioneers relied instead on their prophet/leader. As for Harris' description of Salt Lake Valley, Clayton

Brigham Young's Forest Farm Home, Pioneer Trail State Park, Salt Lake City
Bryan Davies

added, *"We feel we shall know best by going ourselves."*

The next day, June 28, no less an authority than Jim Bridger met the party after it crossed the Big Sandy. The long-anticipated conversation with the builder of Fort Bridger was less than satisfactory. Whiskey had loosened Bridger's tongue, and his long, rambling description of the country, Clayton observed, was *"very imperfect and irregular"*. He did manage to convey his conviction that Utah Valley would be a better place to settle than Salt Lake Valley, and he did speak of cold nights that would make it difficult to grow corn—though no one present recorded anything like the legendary offer of a thousand dollars for the first bushel of corn grown there. Again, Clayton observed that *"We shall know more about things and have a better understanding when we have seen the country ourselves."*

They would receive still more advice. Two days later, while the pioneers were building rafts to cross the Green River, Samuel Brannan rode into camp. Brannan was a trusted Mormon leader who had taken a shipload of Mormons aboard the *Brooklyn* around the Horn to the San Francisco Bay area the previous year. His reports of that country were enthusiastic. Oats grew wild, he reported, barley grew without hulls, and there were fields of clover up to a horse's belly. Throughout his prosperous later career in California and to his death in poverty, there is no evidence he ever understood Brigham's stubborn insistence on settling instead in the empty—but safely isolated—Salt Lake Valley.

It took five days to raft across the Green River and get underway—a welcome relief after suffering swarms of mosquitoes *"more numerous,"* Clayton wrote, *"than I ever saw them anywhere."* Adding to their burdens, the mysterious ailment they called *"mountain fever"* had struck the camp. Brigham had not yet been felled, but soon would be.

Two long days on the trail brought the company to Fort Bridger on July 7. The roadometer showed 397 miles from Fort Laramie, which they had left thirty-three days before.

Trading at the Fort was disappointing; prices were too high, and they could not replenish supplies as they had anticipated. But Wilford Woodruff improved his time by trying, for the first time, some dry flies he had brought from England. In beautiful Blacks Fork, he soon caught twelve trout averaging three-quarters of a pound, while, he boasted, *"The rest of the camp* [using grasshoppers and meat] *did not catch three pounds all together. This is proof that the artificial fly is best to fish with"*—initiating an argument that has not been settled to this day.

From Fort Bridger, they faced the last 100 miles of the trail, the part in Utah and through the Wasatch Mountains. No longer could they follow the dusty but well-traveled Oregon or California trails; from here on, only the dim tracks left the previous year by the Donners and others would show the way. It was time to get out the picks and shovels and axes; there was road-building to be done.

The next two days showed what they were in for. Up and down ridges so steep, Thomas Bullock wrote, that *"it seemed like jumping off the roof of a house;"* digging and chopping and locking wheels and holding back wagons with ropes; taking elevations and barometric pressures and drawing maps to help the groups that would follow—this would be the daily labor until they reached the valley.

July 11 was a Sunday with time to rest and explore—and get more advice. On that day, a few miles southeast of present-day Evanston, in the middle of what would be known as the Overthrust Belt, John Norton discovered oil bubbling to the surface in a black spring. The pioneers used it to grease wagon wheels. On the same day, Miles Goodyear appeared and tried to persuade Brigham to settle near his cabin in the Ogden area. He failed. *"We have an idea he is anxious to have us make a road to his place through selfish motives,"* Clayton wrote.

In another day, they crossed the Bear River and pushed up Coyote Creek to camp almost exactly on what would be the Utah state line. It was here that "Mountain Fever" felled Brigham Young, leaving him, Heber C. Kimball reported, *"insensible and raving."*

With Brigham too sick to travel, Kimball took charge. The company would divide into three groups, he decided. An advance party of twenty-three wagons and forty-three men under Orson Pratt would move ahead, scout the route, and rough out a road. The main party would follow and improve the road. Brigham and the others who had the fever would follow as best they could.

Pratt described Echo Canyon, which his party reached near present-day Wahsatch, as *"a narrow valley ten to twenty rods wide,*

Left: Echo Canyon. From the Lynn Fausett Mormon Trail painting, Pioneer Trail State Park, Salt Lake City
Courtesy Fiametta Fausett

Right: Descending Big Mountain, Salt Lake Valley in the background. From the Lynn Fausett Mormon Trail painting, Pioneer Trail State Park, Salt Lake City
Courtesy Fiametta Fausett

while on each side the hills rise very abruptly 800 to 1,200 feet.'' The going was rough, he complained, with the road repeatedly crossing the creek in the bottom. But their road work was effective enough that the main party made twenty-five miles in one day's travel down the canyon, even while taking time to enjoy this first experience with Utah scenery.

Clayton called Echo Canyon more *''romantic and more interesting''* than any place he had seen. He recorded how the canyon got its name: *"A rifle shot resembles a sharp crack of thunder and echoes back and forth for some time. The lowing of cattle and the braying of mules seems to be answered beyond the mountains . . . music, especially brass instruments, have a very pleasing effect.''*

Still, there was general relief when they made camp where Echo Canyon empties into the broad valley of the Weber River. The interchanges of I-80 and I-84 now cover the spot.

The advance company had no time to play with echoes in the canyon. It had pushed another five miles down the Weber to Devils Slide, where the cliffs crowd close to the river's edge and the water tumbles over great boulders through the narrow slot. It was here, a year earlier, that the Harlan-Young party had begun its ordeal of winching its wagons over the cliffs to negotiate the ten-mile Weber Narrows, and here that the Heinrich Lienhard party had put its wagons right into the stream bed and driven down the foaming torrent.

But the Mormons were looking for some-

thing else—Reed's Cutoff, the trail left the year before by the Donner-Reed party in following Lansford Hasting's recommended route through the Wasatch. On July 15, they found it, a dim, grass-grown track that turned south from the river near present Henefer.

Here began the final thirty-six miles of trail, the hardest of all. It took the Donner-Reed party sixteen days to travel those miles, a delay that cost half of them their lives in the Sierras. The main party of Mormons did it in just four days, thanks to road work done by the Donners and to a great deal of road improvement by the advance party.

The first six miles were up a broad ravine that led to Hogsback Ridge; they called it Main Canyon. Just short of the summit, a rod or two west of Highway 65, deep ruts cut in the bedrock are the best physical evidence of the thousands of wagons that followed Reed's Cutoff.

From the summit, the pioneers got their first good look at what they faced. *"The country west looks rough and mountainous,"* Clayton understated. Rough it was. Clayton described the seven- mile descent down Dixie Hollow into East Canyon:

" . . . arrived at the summit of Hogsback and put a guide board up, '80 miles to Fort Bridger' . . . the descent is not very steep but exceedingly dangerous to wagons, being mostly on the side hill over large cobble stones, causing the wagons to slide very badly [and a number of them to suffer collapsed wheels] *. . . at two o'clock we halted beside a small creek* [Dixie Creek] *to water teams . . . at 3:35 we started forward, the road turning suddenly to the right for about*

Above: "Echo Canyon—Utah"
by nineteenth-century artist
William Henry Jackson.
Courtesy Utah State Historical Society

Pioneer woman and child. From
the Lynn Fausett Mormon Trail
painting, Pioneer Trail State Park,
Salt Lake City
Courtesy Fiametta Fausett

three-quarters of a mile and then a southwest course again. Here we ascended a very long steep hill for nearly a mile, then descended by a very crooked road. I think a better road might be made here and this high hill avoided and save a mile's travel." But it would be many years before a road was cut all the way through Dixie Hollow.

For the next eight miles, up East Canyon Creek, all journals agree that the greatest abomination was the almost impenetrable willow thickets that filled the valley floor. Orson Pratt, leading the advance company, wrote:

"We followed the dimly traced wagon tracks up this stream for 8 miles, crossing the same 13 times. The bottoms of this creek are thickly covered with willows . . . making an immense labor in cutting a road through for the emigrants last season. We still found the road almost impassable, and requiring much labor."

Clayton described tangles of willows and brush twenty feet high. "Although there has been a road cut through, it is scarcely possible to travel without tearing the wagon covers," he wrote, adding that where the willows had been cut, the stubs still made it "very severe on the wagons"—to say nothing of the feet of men and animals. Norton Jacob, while crediting the work done by the Pioneer Company, added dryly, "there is room for more labor."

The willows served one useful purpose. Springs along East Canyon Creek create marshes that make hiking there impracticable even today. The pioneers took their wagons through such places on roads built by laying vast quantities of willows in the muck.

While Brigham Young and others were suffering twenty-two miles behind on the Weber and the main party was struggling with the East Canyon willows, Orson Pratt, scouting ahead for the advance party, climbed Big Mountain with John Brown. Looking past one more mountain range to where a light blue sky "seemed to be sinking into a plain of gold," they saw level ground at last. This was to be home.

Two more days and they would be there. On July 21, Pratt and Erastus Snow, riding and tying one horse down Emigration Canyon, reached the point where Donner Hill juts down from the south at the canyon mouth. On foot, they followed the Donner-Reed tracks up that steep, dangerous obstacle. Reaching the top, they were rewarded by that sudden view of the broad valley that still astonishes motorists reaching the valley from the east.

"We could not refrain from a shout of joy which almost involuntarily escaped from our lips the moment this grand and lovely scenery was in our view," Pratt wrote. If he and Snow didn't swing their hats, as the legend says, and shout "Hosannah! Hosannah! Hosannah!", they should have. But there was much yet to do that day. Still sharing the lone horse, Pratt and Snow made a twelve-mile circuit around the valley before hurrying back up the canyon to report what life would be like in their new home.

On that same day, the main party performed a feat of travel that any modern hiker on the trail must find hard to believe. Eager to catch up with the advance company and

enter the valley together, they pulled out of their camp on the eastern foot of Big Mountain at 6:30 a.m. The oxen were fresh and well-fed on East Canyon's lush grass, but Big Mountain is a stiff 4.5-mile uphill grind, and it gets really steep near the top.

"Much time was necessarily spent cutting down tree stumps, heaving out rocks and leveling the road," William Clayton wrote. "It is an exceedingly rough place."

But not as rough, or as steep, as the going down. On all the trail from Winter Quarters, there are few places as steep as the west face of Big Mountain—and nowhere is it as steep for so long. Straight down the slope the wagons plunged, dragging logs and with wheels locked to prevent runaways. A deeply eroded gully marks the route today.

Clayton wasn't much impressed by the work done by the advance party on Big Mountain: "We found the road down exceedingly steep and rendered dangerous by the many stumps of trees left standing in the road. The brethren cut many of them, which delayed us much."

Through the dense oak and maple thickets of Mountain Dell, crossing that creek twelve times in five miles, they reached a beautiful campsite at the foot of Little Mountain, soon to be covered by water backed up behind Little Dell Dam. But there would be no camping there this day, even after ten hours of strenuous travel.

Years of taking youth groups over the trail have taught me never to climb Little Mountain in the afternoon. Especially in July. There is no shade here, and youngsters fade and sometimes faint in the stiffness of the climb.

Mormon pioneers first viewed the Salt Lake Valley from the pass at Big Mountain. From the Lynn Fausett Mormon Trail painting, Pioneer Trail State Park, Salt Lake City

Courtesy Fiametta Fausett

Yet, the pioneers and their animals, already badly worn by ten hours of toil, tackled that slope in the hottest part of a July day. Tersely, Clayton's journal records that before they reached the summit, *"some of the teams began to fail."*

Wheels were rough-locked again for a mile down the west slope to Emigration Creek. There, after covering fourteen killing miles in thirteen hours, weary men fell into bedrolls in the last camp of the 110-day journey.

With all respect to Brigham Young and today's 24th of July celebration, July 22 was the climactic day for the Saints. In the morning, the advance party reached the point, just above the canyon's mouth, where Donner Hill juts out from the south rim and the canyon pinches into a narrow slot blocked by a tangle of timber and boulders. They could plainly see the tracks left by the Donner-Reed wagons as they struggled up the hill to avoid this final obstacle.

But the Mormons had a different mission. They were building a road for the future, and anyone could see that this steep, narrow, dangerous ridge was no place for that. They acted characteristically. After a brief scouting mission showed it could be done, Mormon axes, shovels and prybars went to work, and in four hours a road was finished through the canyon bottom.

Meanwhile, the main party had twisted its way down Emigration Creek, crossing it nineteen times in those 4.5 miles. The two groups rolled into the valley only a couple of hours apart and were reunited in camp that night on Parleys Creek at about 17th South and 5th East. Only a recuperating

Brigham and a few wagons escorting him remained behind.

For Brigham as well as for those already in the valley, July 23 was a long day. Brigham and his group covered the same fourteen miles that had so exhausted the main party—over Big Mountain, down Mountain Dell Creek, and over Little Mountain to Emigration Canyon. Ten hours it took them on the improved road, including a two-hour rest stop at what is now Birch Springs campground.

In the valley, the pioneers moved to a camp on City Creek. There had always been a duality about their movement—a spirituality, looking to God, and a practicality, looking to their own organized and disciplined strength. On the day their journey ended and the roots went down, it was the same. At what would become State Street and Third South, they assembled, Thomas Bullock wrote, and offered *"a prayer of thanks to the Almighty for the preservation of the camp, their prosperity in the journey and their safe arrival in this place . . .* [and] *consecrated and dedicated the land to the Lord."* Hard upon the last *"Amen"*, they were breaking plows in the sun-baked soil.

Before that day was over, they had thrown a dam across City Creek, dug ditches to bring water to flood and soften the land, and marked off and plowed garden patches. Potatoes would be in the ground the next day. Whatever Brigham would or would not say when he arrived, they well understood that this was the place.

Historians doubt that Brigham made that famous statement about the place he had

ordeal. These were members of the Willie and Martin handcart companies, central figures in the most tragic, heroic chapter of all those written on the Mormon Trail.

But how did they come to be on those high plains in such condition? What motivation sent that many people—men and women, children and toddlers and infants in arms, grey-haired grandmothers and women long into their pregnancy—pulling and pushing two-wheeled carts into the teeth of a Wyoming winter? The answer lay in that epic of faith and obedience known as The Gathering.

Hardly had the pioneers arrived in Salt Lake Valley before the word spread through Mormondom to gather there. This was to be their place of refuge, their New Jerusalem, the center of Zion. But many, particularly European converts, were too poor to come on their own. To help them, Brigham Young established a revolving fund, loans from which were to be repaid after the converts were established in their new homes.

The emigrants drew heavily on the Perpetual Emigration Fund, and the numbers grew. The flood reached a peak in 1855, just as a drought and plague of grasshoppers left Zion in economic distress. With the fund depleted and thousands of converts clamoring to come, Brigham proposed a solution:

"We cannot purchase wagons and teams as in years past. I am consequently thrown back on my old plan—to make handcarts and let the emigration foot it . . . They can come just as quick, if not quicker, and much cheaper—can start earlier and escape the prevailing sickness which annually lays so

many of our brethren in the dust."

With characteristic Mormon efficiency, the program was launched. Church agents in England arranged ship passage for the immigrants. Others in Iowa City, Iowa, arranged to build the handcarts and organize and outfit the companies.

The disaster that struck the two companies in Wyoming has led many to conclude that the plan was foolhardy, if not insane. It wasn't. Three handcart companies with a total of 815 men, women, and children left Iowa City in mid-June 1856. The first reached Salt Lake Valley in 109 days, the others in comparable time. Twenty persons died on the trail. Both in time spent on the trail and in casualties en route, these handcart companies compared favorably with the traditional wagon trains. So did five other companies that came by handcart between 1857 and 1860.

Altogether, some 3,000 emigrants made their way west in handcart companies. Except for those in the Willie and Martin companies, they left some forty-five graves along the trail—a remarkably low number for those times.

These Mormons were received in the valley as heroes. Edmund Ellsworth, captain of the first company, recorded its arrival:

"About eight miles from the city we were met with Governor Young and his counselors, the Nauvoo brass band, the Lancers, and a great many others. We were first rate received in the city. Provisions of all kinds came rolling in to us in camp. The brethren of the city manifested great interest towards us as a company, which caused our hearts

to rejoice and be glad."

Heroes and heroines they were indeed, as I have had occasion to reflect while watching husky, well-fed teenagers try to manhandle lightly loaded and well-greased handcarts over Big Mountain. How the pioneers managed theirs, loaded with all their earthly belongings, while carrying an infant or leading a toddler by the hand, is beyond modern understanding—especially considering the quality of their carts. Captain Daniel D. McArthur of the second company described them:

"Our carts, when we started, were in an awful fix. They moaned and growled, screeched and squealed, so that a person could hear them for miles . . . we had them to eternally patch, mornings, noons and nights. But by our industry we got them all along to Florence . . . went to work and gave our carts a thorough repair throughout, and on the 24th of July, at 12 o'clock, we struck our tents and started for the plains, all in the best of spirits." With this and a thousand other examples of faith, courage, and determination, the handcart pioneers justified Brigham's faith in his people.

Tragically, it was the two largest companies that were struck by disaster. Delayed in sailing and again in outfitting, the company led by returning missionary James G. Willie did not leave Iowa City until July 15; the Edward Martin Company left thirteen days later. Both companies had been warned that it was far too late in the season to start and that they faced grave risks. But enthusiasm for The Gathering was high, and they voted to proceed, having faith that

Mormon youth coax a handcart up Big Mountain during an outing in which they re-traced the Mormon Trail from East Canyon to the Salt Lake Valley.
Kevin Stoker

the weather would be tempered.

It wasn't. The first winter storm, much earlier than usual, hit on October 19, just as the Martin Company was becoming thoroughly soaked in the last crossing of the Platte near present-day Casper, Wyoming. People started dying almost immediately, and the deaths mounted daily in both companies as blizzards swept the plains and temperatures plummeted far below zero. Starving, exhausted, and freezing, the survivors could only huddle in their bitter camps along the Sweetwater, praying for rescue.

The dramatic rescue effort was a model of Mormon organization, discipline, and efficiency. Brigham Young first learned on October 4 that the handcart companies were still on the Wyoming plains. He sensed the coming disaster. The Mormons' October General Conference began two days later, and his sermon to the opening session

was brief and to the point:

"Many of our brethren and sisters are on the plains with handcarts and we must send assistance to them . . . That is my religion; that is the dictation of the Holy Ghost that I possess. It is to save the people . . . I will tell you that your faith, religion, and profession of religion, will never save one soul of you in the Celestial Kingdom of our God, unless you carry out just such principles as I am now teaching you. Go and bring in those people now on the plains."

Harvey Cluff, who had walked the forty-five miles from Provo to attend the conference, heard the message. He wrote:

"The response to the call of President Young was most remarkable. On the following day, Oct. 7, 22 teams—two span of mules or horses to each wagon and each wagon loaded to the bows. There were about 50 young men in the company. Being in Salt

Lake City and of an ambitious turn of mind, I volunteers to go."

And he went, as did hundreds of others. By the end of October, 250 relief wagons had rolled up Emigration Canyon. By early November the rescuers had the survivors moving again, most of them riding in wagons. But the ordeal was not ended—nor was the heroism. Three eighteen-year-old boys in the rescue company carried nearly every member of the Martin company across the Sweetwater River on their backs, suffering such exposure that all three were soon dead.

In a dispatch to Brigham Young from the disaster site, George D. Grant, who led the first rescue train, described the tragedy:

" . . . you can imagine between five and six hundred men, women and children, worn down by drawing handcarts through snow and mud; fainting by the wayside; fall-

ing, chilled by the cold; children crying, their *l*imbs stiffened by cold, their feet bleeding *a*nd some of them bare to snow and frost. *T*he sight is almost too much for the stoutest *o*f us . . .

"Our company is too small to help much, *i*t is only a drop to a bucket, as it were, in *c*omparison to what is needed. I think that *n*ot over one-third of br. Martin's company *i*s able to walk . . . Some of them have good *c*ourage and are in good spirits; but a great *m*any are like children and do not help *t*hemselves much more, nor realize what is *b*efore them . . .

"Br. Charles Decker has now traveled this *r*oad the 49th time, and he says he has never *b*efore seen so much snow on the Sweet *W*ater at any season of the year . . .

"We will move every day toward the val-*l*ey, if we shovel snow to do it, the Lord help-*i*ng us."

The spirit with which the survivors were greeted when they reached the valley reflected a speech by Brigham at a special meeting in the Tabernacle on November 30. He spoke of the imminent arrival of the wagons carrying the Martin company:

"When those persons arrive I do not want to see them put into houses by themselves; I want to have them distributed in the city among the families that have good and comfortable houses; and I wish all the sisters now before me, and all who know how and can, to nurse and wait upon the new comers and prudently administer medicine and food to them. To speak upon these things is a part of my religion, for it pertains to taking care of the Saints . . .

"The afternoon meeting will be omitted, for I wish the sisters to go home and prepare to give those who have just arrived a mouthful of something to eat, and to wash them and nurse them up. You know that I would give more for a dish of pudding and milk, or a baked potato and salt, were I in the situation of those persons who have just come in, than I would for all your prayers, though you were to stay here all the afternoon and pray. Prayer is good, but when baked potatoes and pudding and milk are needed, prayer will not supply their place . . .

"Some you will find with their feet frozen to their ankles; some are frozen to their knees and some have their hands frosted . . . we want you to receive them as your own children and to have the same feeling for them."

The Saints complied, then and in the years to follow. Of all who trekked the Mormon Trail, none enjoyed—or deserve—more honor than those who did it this hardest of all ways.

Mormon youth and handcart near the top of Big Mountain
Kevin Stoker

Mormon youth descend Big Mountain during a trek along a portion of the Mormon Trail.
Kevin Stoker

Mountain Meadows, a favorite campsite on the Spanish Trail. Jefferson Hunt led his small party through here after most of his train had split off on what they believed to be a shortcut to California. Many ended up in Death Valley.
Scott T. Smith

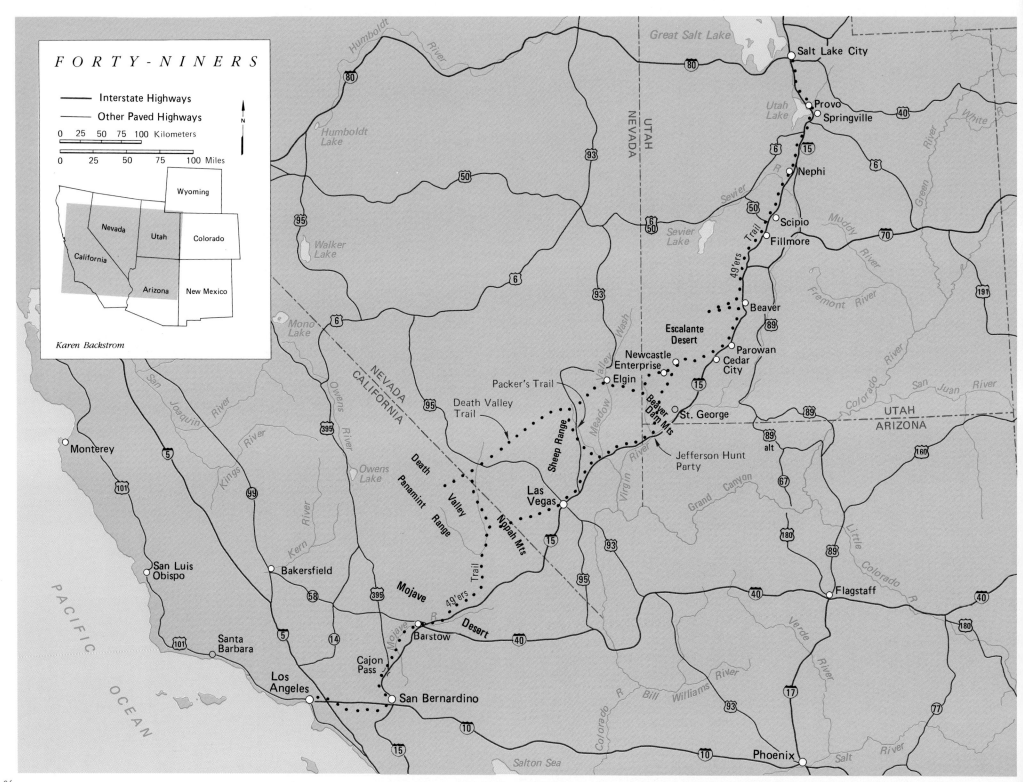

FORTY-NINERS

Interstate Highways
Other Paved Highways

N

0   25   50   75   100 Kilometers

0   25   50   75   100 Miles

Wyoming
Nevada   Utah   Colorado
California
Arizona   New Mexico

Karen Backstrom

Great Salt Lake

Salt Lake City

UTAH
NEVADA

Provo
Springville

Humboldt River

Humboldt Lake

Nephi

Scipio

Fillmore

49'ers Trail

Beaver

Escalante Desert

Newcastle
Enterprise
Elgin

Parowan
Cedar City

Packer's Trail

Death Valley Trail

Sheep Range

Beaver Dam Mts

St. George

Jefferson Hunt Party

UTAH
ARIZONA

Walker Lake

Mono Lake

Las Vegas

Death Valley

Panamint Range

Owens Lake

Nopah Mts

49'ers Trail

Grand Canyon

Monterey

Owens River

Bakersfield

Mojave

Desert

Barstow

Mojave R

Cajon Pass

49'ers Trail

San Luis Obispo

Santa Barbara

Los Angeles

San Bernardino

Flagstaff

PACIFIC OCEAN

Phoenix

Salton Sea

Salt River

94

FORTY-NINERS

The long trail that was to become I-15 from Salt Lake City to Los Angeles took shape piece by piece over three-quarters of a century. The first white men on the trail were Fathers Dominguez and Escalante, who traveled in 1776 from Utah Lake to present-day Scipio before they struck out to the west into the Escalante Desert. In the same year, Father Garces discovered the south end of the trail.

Mountain Man Jedediah Smith filled in most of the vast space between in 1826 and again, with variations, in 1827. Trappers Ewing Young, Kit Carson, Peter Skene Ogden, and others followed parts of the trail over the next few years. The New Mexican traders, Young and Wolfskill, made the first complete trip in 1830 over what became the Spanish Trail. They were followed in the next two decades by traders driving uncounted thousands of mules and horses. From Parowan south, theirs was the well-defined trail to Los Angeles. Fremont mapped the country up to Utah Lake in 1844. Miles Goodyear, having sold his trading post near Ogden to the Mormons, took a pack train over the entire Salt Lake-Los Angeles trail in 1848.

So, the route was well known, but only as a horse trail. It remained for boys of the Mormon Battalion, mustered out in San Diego in 1848, to manhandle the first wagon over the trail. But it was California-bound Forty-Niners led by other Mormons the following year who cut and dug the horse trail into a real wagon road.

H. G. Boyle led twenty-five men of the Mormon Battalion party who declined to re-enlist after the Mexican-American war. Finally mustered out, they left for Salt Lake Valley in March 1848 with 135 mules. They loaded a wagon with fruit cuttings and grain from the prosperous California ranches and managed to drag it through to Salt Lake by June 5.

That was just the beginning. The real wagon traffic started the following year, 1849, when thousands of gold-seekers headed for California. Many emigrants reached Salt Lake Valley too late to push on to California by way of the Humboldt River and the Sierras. The fate of the Donner-Reed party was too well-known to risk starting so late. But the prospect of wintering among the Mormons was not appealing, either. No work was to be had there, and lurid tales of Mormon violence toward the "Gentiles" had spread along the trail.

Captain Jefferson Hunt of the Mormon Battalion offered an alternative. He had been twice over the southern route and would guide gold-seekers to Los Angeles for $10 a wagon. But, he advised, they should wait for cooler weather. While they waited, they could fatten their oxen in the lush meadows of Utah Valley and get ready for the long, thirsty drive. Some 500 emigrants with 100 wagons accepted the offer. Among them was Lewis Manly, who had narrowly escaped with his life after a foolhardy attempt to float down the Green River to California. Many painful months later, he would be a central figure in rescuing some of the party from Death Valley.

Some emigrants were unable or unwilling to pay Hunt's fee and pushed off on their own with twenty-three wagons. They did not fare well. Hunt caught up with them later, broken down and starving, in the Mojave Desert. He was able to give them enough provisions to save their lives.

Rested, those who had cast their fate with Hunt set out from present-day Springville on October 2, but only after Hunt had told them what to expect. *"He described the route with the roughest side out,"* James Brown recalled, *"lest they might say that he had misled them by making things more favorable than they really were. In concluding his remarks, he warned: 'From Salt Springs, we cross to a sandy desert, distance seventy-five miles to Bitter Springs, the water so bitter the devil would not drink it; and from thence away hellwards, to California or some other place. Now, gentlemen, if you will stick together and follow me, I will lead you through to California all right; but you will have to make your own road . . . ' "*

Make their own road they did. Stick together they didn't, with tragic consequences.

In sixteen days, the party traveled 175 miles to Beaver Creek, closely paralleling today's I-15. There were complaints about the dust, and reports about the vast swarms of jack rabbits. *"Had fine sport killing mountain hare,"* Sheldon Young's log reports. Lewis Manly adds that in one valley, probably around Scipio, they killed 500 rabbits. There were sage hens to be shot, too, and fish to catch.

On Chalk Creek at the site of present-day Fillmore, Young's log notes: *"Discovered the ruins of an ancient city. There was earthenware and glass. It was five miles in extent."* These would have been remnants of the

View from the Kolob Plateau overlooking Cedar Valley, through which the Forty-Niners passed on their way to California.
John George

Fremont culture, which had vanished from the area 800 years earlier.

Near present-day Beaver, twenty Mormon missionaries with two wagons, on their way to the Hawaiian islands, caught up with the wagon train. J. M. Flake headed this company, but the real leader would be Apostle Charles C. Rich. The train was also joined by twenty non-Mormon packers led by Captain O. K. Smith.

It was here the troubles began.

The first bad judgment seems to have been by Hunt himself. He had heard of a shortcut to the west, he reported, and was willing to try it. He knew very little about it, he emphasized, and would not be responsible for the outcome. But he had planted the seed, and the party voted to go.

Twelve miles down Beaver Creek they moved and camped, then another twelve miles across a dry and dusty plain. There, in a dry camp, they waited Hunt's return from scouting the country ahead. At about midnight the second day, he rode into camp, almost dead with thirst and with bad news.

James S. Brown, one of the mission-bound Mormons, recorded: *"Sometime in the night Captain Hunt came into camp, so near choked from lack of water that his tongue was swollen till it protruded from his mouth; his eyes were so sunken in his head that he could scarcely be recognized. His horse, too, for the need of water, was blind, and staggered as he was urged on. Their stay had been thirty-six hours, on the sands, without water."*

Hunt had pushed forty miles out into the Escalante Desert, he reported, and that was no way to go; the country was far too dry. Sullen and angry, the company retraced its steps. They had lost seven days on the supposed shortcut and began to wonder if Hunt

knew what he was doing. Some wondered whether the trip was really just a ruse to get them to build a wagon road for the Mormons.

"A general commotion was visible or rather a rebellion," Addison Pratt wrote in his diary. *"Slurs were frequently thrown out about the Mormons and some even went so far as to threaten Capt. Hunt's life if they did not get through safely and the greatest unreasonableness was shown by them. Bro Hunt began to feel that his case was very uncertain among them as they expressed themselves determined to blame him for*

every mishap even when it was a matter that did not concern him at all."

In such a climate, Captain O.K. Smith, leader of the packers, found ready listeners for a new idea. He produced a map supposedly drawn by Mountain Man Bill Williams and obtained from Barney Ward, another early trapper. It showed, he said, a real short-cut heading straight west to Walker's Pass in the Sierras. It would cut 500 miles from the trip; they would be in the gold fields in twenty days.

There was hot argument during the next nine days of travel past Little Salt Lake [near

present-day Parowan], where they joined the Spanish Trail; then west over the Antelope Range and around the fringe of the Escalante Desert to Pinto Creek near Newcastle. Now it was time for decision.

A general meeting was called. In the company were several preachers, including J. W. Brier, a Methodist who, Pratt wrote, *"liked to give his opinion on every subject . . . He took the opportunity to fire the minds of the people with a zeal for the cut off and closed by saying that the road across the deserts they know to be a bad one but they did not know what the road on the cut off was but*

Forty-Niners reported swarms of jack rabbits in sage flats such as these below the San Pitch Mountains.
John George

hoped it was a good one and go it he should sink or swim, live or die . . . "

Others spoke in much the same way. Then it was Hunt's turn. He told them, according to non-Mormon Jacob Stover: *"Gentlemen, I agreed to pilot you through and if only one wagon goes with me I will go with it. If you want to follow Captain Smith, I can't help it, but I believe you will get into the jaws of hell; but I hope you will have good luck."*

Pratt reported it a little differently. According to his diary, Hunt told the group that *"he had never been the cut off, nor had never seen anybody that had been it, therefore, he could tell nothing about it. They then took a vote to see how many would go the cut off. Nearly all of them voted in favour of it to the great satisfaction of Capt. Hunt."*

That last remark seems curious, but Pratt's journal explains it: *"After we had divided into two companies, each company stopped to bid the other adieu and as we began to give each other the parting hand, Bro. Hunt put on a very long face as if he were about to shed tears . . . He told them that his contract was to pilot them across the desert and as long as there was one wagon that wished to go that way he was obliged to go with them . . .*

"Not long after he came on and overtook us I laughed at him a little for his crocodile tears . . . 'This,' he said, 'is the happiest day of my life. I cannot recollect the time when I made so lucky an escape from death before as I have in getting rid of this company. There is a certain set of mobocratic spirits among them that were determined to take

my life before we should get through the deserts. Now we will travel on fast as possible and get out of their way for they will soon be coming on after us when their cattle begin to die for there is neither grass nor water that way."

Whatever Hunt's motives, the defection was almost complete. Only seven wagons stayed with him. On November 4, a hundred wagons and all of the packers turned west on the cutoff, but only after some of the more enthusiastic among them bored holes in trees, filled them with gunpowder and exploded them in celebration of the breakup of the party. A stone marker, hidden away off a dirt road five miles east of Newcastle, marks the point of separation.

Apostle Rich and his party of Mormon missionaries went with the defectors. Missionary James Brown, a Mormon Battalion veteran who was at Sutters Mill when gold was discovered there, attempted to explain why. In reminiscences written fifty years later, he said:

"Brother Rich told me that it had been shown to him that there was going to be trouble, and he felt led to believe that if we would go with the pack train he could at least lead the brethren there back on to the trail and save them. This was in the night, as we slept together in the wagon. He awoke and asked me if I were awake. Finding that I was, he told me what should befall the company. To save the brethren and all who would heed him, he purchased some ponies and went with the packers."

Brown's account does not square with others that tell of Rich's initial enthusiasm for

I-15 through Cedar Valley follows the route of the Spanish Trail and the Forty-Niners
Frank Jensen

the new route. But whatever his reasons, it turned out that he did lead many back to the trail.

Hunt and his small group plodded forward on the well-known Spanish Trail, through Mountain Meadows, and over the Great Basin rim to the Virgin River. They crossed the seemingly endless Mormon Flats to the springs at Las Vegas, across southern Nevada to the NoPah (no water) mountains, which they crossed over Emigrant Pass to Resting Spring and the Amargosa River. Then they attacked the Jornada del Muerte, the bone-littered, waterless eighty-mile stretch to the Mojave, and finally over Cajon Pass. On December 22, they reached the vineyards and orchards and fat cattle of Williams Ranch in San Bernardino Valley. Along the way, many of those who had abandoned the shortcut had rejoined Hunt and made the trip safely.

For those who followed Captain Smith on the cutoff, Hunt's prediction proved to be prophetic. They did, indeed, go into the jaws of hell.

But not at first. Heading straight west through present Enterprise and up Shoal Creek, they found three days of pleasant traveling. This is lovely country, with a fairly wide, easy valley, fringed with the red rock so beautifully typical of southern Utah. A dirt road now roughly follows the trail, climbing through pinyon-juniper country onto a 7,000-foot plateau.

Nineteen miles up Shoal Creek, the group turned southwest up White Rocks Wash. They reached what is now the Dixie National Forest, near where the Iron-Washington

County line meets the Utah-Nevada border. Here began the trials Hunt had predicted. Manly's account is the most descriptive:

"Immediately in front of us was a canyon, impassable for wagons, and down into this the trail descended. Men could go, horses and mules, perhaps, but wagons could no longer follow that trail, and we proposed to camp while explorers were sent out to search a pass across this steep and rocky canyon. Wood and bunch grass were plenty, but water was a long way down the trail and had to be packed up to the camp."

They had reached the rim of the Great Basin and dead-ended against the headwaters of Beaver Dam Wash, which runs in an ever-deepening gorge off this high plateau roughly along the Utah-Nevada border all the way into what is now Arizona.

Manly continued: *"Two days passed, and the parties sent out began to come in, all reporting no way to go farther with wagons. Some said the trail on the west side of the canyon could be ascended on foot by both men and mules, but that it would take years to make it fit for wheels.*

"The enthusiasm about the Smith cutoff had begun to die and now the talk began of going back to follow Hunt. On the third morning a lone traveler with a small wagon and one yoke of oxen, died . . . He was decently buried by the men of the company.

"This very morning a Mr. Rynierson called the attention of the crowd and made some remarks upon the situation. He said: 'My family is near and dear to me. I can see by the growth of the timber that we are in a very elevated place . . . We are evidently

in a country where snow is liable to fall at any time in the winter season, and if we were to remain here and be caught in a severe storm we should all probably perish. I, for one, feel in duty bound to seek a safer way than this. I shall hitch up my oxen and return at once to the old trail. Boys [to his teamsters] *get the cattle and we'll return.'"*

That started a general exodus back to the original trail. Stover's journal calls the place Mount Misery. It could well be called Mount Separation, because here the party was fragmented.

Those who followed Rynierson back to the Spanish Trail left little record of their journey, but seem to have reached California with only the expected suffering and thirst. So did Apostle Rich's missionary party and most of the packers who started out with Captain Smith. Another group abandoned their wagons at Mount Misery, packed their belongings on mules and oxen, and pushed on. Finally, twenty-five wagons went ten miles north around the head of Beaver Dam Wash and made entirely new tracks west across Nevada and into Death Valley. These are the stubborn unfortunates whose suffering and tragedy gave Death Valley its name.

We can follow, briefly, the fortunes of each group:

Together with Captain Smith's group, Apostle Rich and his missionary packers left the wagon train and found a way into Beaver Dam Wash. Henry W. Bigler, a Mormon Battalion veteran on his way to the Hawaiian mission, kept a diary of their journey.

The second day in the bottom of the wash, Bigler wrote, he carved his initials and the date, November 3, in the rock. Eighty-nine years later, historian Charles Kelly had the excitement of finding them. His description was published in the February 1939 *Desert Magazine*:

"We drove back toward White Rock Wash, but before reaching the rim, turned on a very dim trail which soon led us to the brink of the wash. Straight down it ran, apparently into the bowels of the earth, the longest, steepest, narrowest trail we had ever encountered in many years of desert travel. Down, down, and down we went at a snail's pace, finally reaching a small meadow containing an abandoned cabin. Walls of the canyon were of white volcanic ash, so we scrutinized them closely for names. At last to our joy we found deeply engraved the name 'Osborn 49' We knew then we were on the trail of the 49ers. We might find the inscription Bigler said he made!"

They did, a quarter-mile up the wash, but the writing was so dim that after another half-century there would be little trace left.

Travel down Beaver Dam Wash must have been rough. Bigler's journal makes no mention of the long, steep trail that so impressed Kelly, but is sprinkled with such subsequent entries as: *"The Canion narrow in places, dangerous for animals to travil. one place whare we came along today that one false step would plunged a horse hundreds of feet down the mountain . . . it was extremely bad for our animals, being vary rockkey and a precipice to assend . . . It is really surprise-ing to see whare horse can go, some of them fell and rolled over with their packs on, Some we helped up the precipice by putting ropes* round thier necks and 8 or 10 men at the end to pull and so help them up . . . we have no feed in this Canion and no man can think how bad the traveling."*

After three days of this, they left the wash, only to spend the next nine days thirsting their way west across Nevada's deserts and barren mountains. On one afternoon, Bigler wrote, *"2 of my animals give out. one was the best, as I thought . . . here I could of Cried! I pitied the poor dum bruits, leave them without a drop of water to perish or for the indians to kill & eat after serving me so faithful to the vary last until they could go no longer."*

On November 11, Bigler recorded Apostle Rich's increasing impatience with Smith's leadership:

"Bro. Rich said that this kind of travel-ing would not do, that his Council had not been taken, if it had we would not been here and that he was not going to travil this way any longer, if we did we would perish in the mountains. that if he could not have his way he would go back to the waggons as soon as he could."

Five days later, he did. After climbing a mountain in the Sheep Creek range to see what was ahead and finding *"no sight for water or grass as far as he could see,"* Rich made his decision. Bigler recorded the scene:

"Capt Smith came and asked Bro. Rich what discoveries he made from the top of the mountain and what way he thought of going & Bro Rich told him what he had seen and give his opinion of the route, that it was his mind not to go that way any further, that he should make for the Spanish trail. Smith Said he would continue his course a cross the mountain, if he perished and if we never herd from him we mite know he was dead, had died with his face westward and not before he had eaten some mule meat too."*

Rich and his missionaries hurried south, catching up with Hunt just two days short of Las Vegas. As for Smith, he soon changed his mind. Rather than dying with his face turned west and mule meat in his belly, he gave up after only two more days and turned back toward Salt Lake City. Howard Egan, piloting a small train of three wagons, picked him up near Cedar City and took him on to California.

For those who abandoned wagons at Mount Misery and packed on with their horses and oxen, the story is more tragic. Years later, Jacob Y. Stover would remem-ber the separation and how his group had tackled Beaver Dam Wash several days behind Smith and his party. Stover caught up with the captain three weeks later at the base of a high mountain as Smith *"was packing up to go to Salt Lake to winter."*

The outlook wasn't good. Already they were eating horse meat. Some of Stover's party turned back with Smith. Nine others determined to push west across the moun-tain in front of them. Stover did not like two of the men. *"All the way crossing the plains they were on the wrong side every time,"* he wrote. He chose not to go with them, and *"that was what saved me . . . "* Instead, Stover and a few others turned southwest and found the Spanish Trail at the Amargosa River near what would become the Nevada-California border.

View west from Mt. Nebo toward the desert ranges that westering travelers had to cross.
Rick Reese

Stover later learned the fate of the nine men who kept going west. In Nevada City, he met two of them, a Pinney of Ohio and a Savage of Illinois. He recorded their story:

"We went over the mountain and travelled through a rough country, nothing to shoot, not a living thing to be seen, till our horse meat was all gone, and we came one night into a camp on a big desert [apparently west of Death Valley, which they had crossed]. *The boys said we would have to draw cuts in the morning who should be killed to eat. As we did not want to be killed to be eaten or eat anybody, when we thought they were asleep we got up and travelled till day; then we tok our butcher knives and dug holes in the sand and covered up all but our heads till night when we would come out and travel all night again."*

In this way, they reached Owen Lake, where a fishing party of Indians saved them. Skeletons of the other seven men were found later under a brush shelter.

But what about those who stubbornly manhandled their twenty-seven wagons around Beaver Dam Wash and pushed west into the desert? The main group called themselves "The Jayhawkers." They were single men and refused to allow any families to join them. But the vociferous Methodist minister J. W. Brier insisted on tagging along with his family, and so did the J.B. Arcane and A. Bennett families. Also taking this route was a group called the "Georgia Boys" under the leadership of Jim Martin.

From Mount Misery, they headed north, got around the wash, and kept on north, hoping to find the trail supposedly described on Williams' map. Manly kept trying to persuade the Jayhawkers to turn west. The Bennett and Martin groups finally listened and changed course, but the Jayhawkers continued north. In words dripping with smugness, Manly reported that two nights later *"the brave Jayhawkers who had been so firm in going north hove in sight,"* finally convinced that was not the way to California.

The reunited company pushed on through country that got drier with each mile. Twice they captured Indians and tried to force from them information about the right way to go. But one escaped and the other knew nothing. Jayhawker Sheldon Young described the country in his journal: *"There is no running water . . . Grass, it is scarce, wood there is none. It is a dubious looking country."* On November 29 he said the country was *"damned dubious looking,"* and on December 7 it was still *"damned hard looking."*

Their progress was snail-like. Instead of the twenty days promised, it took Young and his group ninety-seven days from the time he left the Spanish Trail to reach safety in San Bernardino Valley, an average of only 3.5 miles a day. For others it was longer. Some never made it at all.

Abandoned wagons, many of them burned to keep them out of Mormon hands, were found later as far as 100 miles east of Death Valley. The Jayhawkers abandoned wagons and packed goods on their oxen in Death Valley, crossed the Panamint Mountains, suffered terribly in the arid country to the southwest, and finally reached safety on February 5. Three of them died enroute.

The Bennett, Arcane, Earhart and Wade families completely bogged down in Death Valley. After two weeks of slow starvation, they decided to send the two strongest men, Manly and John Rogers, to find a way out and, if possible, bring back provisions. It was an heroic effort. They found help at the missions near Los Angeles and returned twenty-six days later with provisions and animals to help carry the starving survivors out. But for some, it was too late. Only the Bennetts with their three children and the Arcanes with their one were left. The Earharts and a Captain Culverwell who had tried to find their own way out died. So, probably, did the Wades.

The two surviving families still had their four wagons when rescue arrived. But they could take them no farther; Manly insisted there was no way a wagon could make it over the trail they had followed. As the forlorn party slogged up the final ridge on the way out of the valley, Mrs. Bennett looked back and, with feelings only to be imagined, uttered the words that have given the region its name: *"Goodby, Death Valley".*

It took this last group four months to complete the *"twenty-day shortcut."* Of the twenty-seven wagons that didn't turn back to the known trail, not one reached its destination. The haggard survivors who did, arrived in Los Angeles with little more than the clothes on their backs. In their eagerness to find a shorter way to the gold fields, they had tried no fewer than ten different routes. Not one was an improvement. The alignment of I-15 almost precisely along Jeff Hunt's trail speaks eloquently of the lesson written by the Forty-Niners.

Snakeweed in flats below Deep Creek Mountains near the Pony Express route

John George

THE PONY EXPRESS

"Across the endless dead level of the prairie, a black speck appears against the sky, and it is plain that it moves. Well I should think so! In a second it becomes a horse and rider, rising and falling, rising and falling—sweeping toward us nearer and nearer, growing more and more distinct, more and more sharply defined—nearer and still nearer, and the flutter of hoofs comes faintly to the ear—another instant a whoop and a hurrah from our upper deck, a wave of the rider's hands but no reply and man and horse burst past our excited faces and go winging away like the belated fragment of a storm!"

So, Mark Twain described his first encounter with a rider of the Pony Express. The romance of his words in *Roughing It* has never faded. The image of flying hoofs spanning half a continent is indelibly etched in western lore.

For followers of Utah's historic trails, there is more than Pony Express lore. There remains also a physical presence—a dirt road that follows the pony tracks a hundred miles over the western Utah desert, some crumbling ruins, a monument or two. But most of all, there is the land—unfenced, unspoiled, unchanged. Is dust destructible? Or is this the same dust pony hoofs sprayed? And the sky—wide, hard, and blue. How many generations of hawks wheeled these skies since those that watched the ponies race by?

To relive western history, you must eat its dust, smell its odors, feel its jolts. There's no better place to do it than along the Pony Express trail to Ibapah. A passenger car will do in good weather. Much better is the back of a horse. Best of all is to get involved with the annual mid-June re-enactment of the ride.

It is hard to find an enterprise more short-lived or more financially ruinous than the Pony Express. For only eighteen months its red-shirted, Bible-carrying riders spurred their mounts over those 1966 miles from St. Joseph, Missouri, to Sacramento, California. In no month did the operation come close to turning an operating profit. And when the final link of the transcontinental telegraph was completed in Salt Lake City on October 24, 1861, the Pony Express was through.

So were its builders; loss of the three-quarters of a million dollars they poured into it completed the bankrupting of what had been one of the West's most powerful firms.

By any practical measure, it was an ill-conceived and utter failure. But some things are bigger than practicalities. Historians of the Pony Express claim it accomplished two things far more important than making a profit for its owners.

First, with the clouds of civil war gathering, it kept California in the Union, ensuring that its gold and Nevada's silver would swell payrolls for men in blue, not grey. Southern sentiment in California had hatched a serious secessionist plot to form a Republic of the Pacific, unite with the Confederacy, and create a Confederate States of America stretching from coast to coast. The conspiracy could have succeeded, given the length of time it took to get messages back and forth from Washington. The Pony Express cut that time in less than half and helped defuse the threat.

Pony Express riders carried Lincoln's inaugural address through to the coast in seven days and seventeen hours—an all-time record—instead of the twenty-five days it took by stage or the four weeks or more by ship and the Isthmus of Panama. News of the firing on Fort Sumter reached California in eight days and fourteen hours, galvanizing Californians to stand firm for the Union.

The second legacy of the Pony Express was the routing of the telegraph, the railroad, and finally the Lincoln Highway across the nation's middle—a fact of great importance to Salt Lake City and Utah. Again, the decision hinged on North-South politics.

In 1857, Congress established and subsidized a transcontinental mail route. Southern congressmen insisted on a southern route, arguing that heavy snows in the Rockies and Sierras made the central route through Fort Laramie and Salt Lake City unreliable and impractical. To no one's surprise, considering the secessionist sentiments in President Buchanan's cabinet, the Southerners won. The route would run southwest from St. Louis to El Paso, on to Albuquerque and Tucson, across the Mojave Desert, and then up the San Joaquin Valley to San Francisco. It was 700 miles longer, but it avoided the winter snows. Unspoken but far more important to the Southerners who controlled Congress was the reality that if war came, the South would control the mail.

The Pony Express changed all that. By keeping to an unbroken schedule through the dead of winter, it proved the central route was practicable. And by establishing transcontinental communication through Free-Soil territory, it stripped from the South one of its potentially greatest assets.

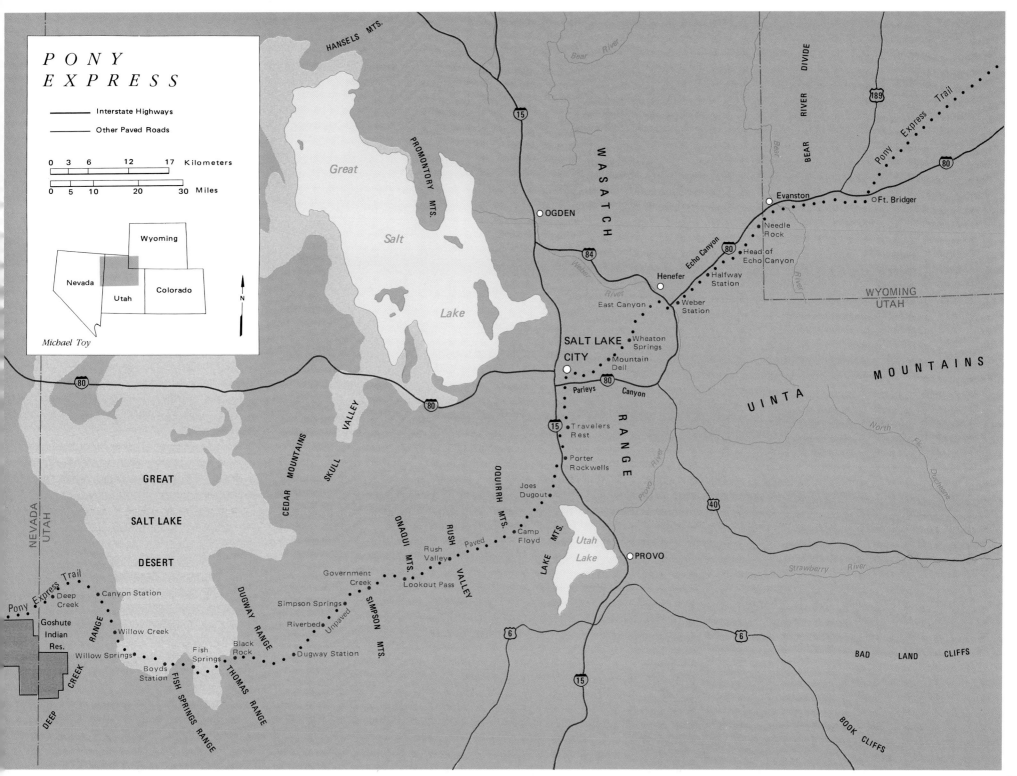

PONY
EXPRESS

Interstate Highways
Other Paved Roads

0 3 6   12   17 Kilometers
0   5   10   20   30 Miles

Nevada
Wyoming
Utah
Colorado

Michael Toy

N

HANSELS MTS.

Bear River

PROMONTORY MTS.

Great

Salt

Lake

OGDEN

WASATCH

15

84

Weber River

Henefer

East Canyon

Weber Station

Echo Canyon

Halfway Station

Head of Echo Canyon

Needle Rock

Evanston

Ft. Bridger

189

80

Pony Express Trail

BEAR RIVER DIVIDE

Bear River

WYOMING
UTAH

SALT LAKE CITY

Wheaton Springs

Mountain Dell

80

Parleys   Canyon

RANGE

UINTA

MOUNTAINS

North Fk.

Duchesne River

15

Travelers Rest

Porter Rockwells

Provo River

40

NEVADA
UTAH

CEDAR MOUNTAINS

SKULL VALLEY

OQUIRRH MTS.

Joes Dugout

Camp Floyd

LAKE MTS.

Utah Lake

PROVO

GREAT

SALT LAKE

DESERT

Pony Express Trail

Deep Creek

Canyon Station

Willow Creek

DUGWAY RANGE

ONAQUI MTS.

Rush Valley

Lookout Pass

Paved

RUSH VALLEY

Government Creek

Strawberry River

Goshute Indian Res.

Willow Springs

Boyds Station

Fish Springs

Black Rock

Simpson Springs

Riverbed

Unpaved

Dugway Station

SIMPSON MTS.

6

6

BAD LAND CLIFFS

15

DEEP CREEK RANGE

FISH SPRINGS RANGE

THOMAS RANGE

BOOK CLIFFS

107

Ironically, the three patriots who accomplished all that for the Union received not a penny and very little thanks from the government. What they mostly got for their efforts was financial ruin.

They were a curious team: William H. Russell, the optimistic, scheming, bantam-size, Washington-wise promoter; William B. Waddell, the hard-headed, practical, bottom-line businessman; and the driving force that made things happen, Alexander Majors, the big, broad-shouldered, teetotalling, Bible-preaching plainsman.

Together, by 1860 they had built the greatest freighting outfit the West had ever seen. Each of their custom-built wagons carried 5,000 to 7,000 pounds of freight. There were 6,250 of them, 75,000 oxen to pull them, and 5,000 men on the payroll to make the whole thing work. One writer estimated that hitched up and in line, the Russell, Majors and Waddell wagons would stretch solidly for forty miles.

This giant enterprise dominated freighting in the West. It carried most of the government contracts to supply the far-flung military outposts, and for many years it freighted supplies to the Mormons in Salt Lake Valley.

One freighting operation to Salt Lake Valley brought the firm to the edge of ruin. That was the 1857 military expedition Secretary of War John B. Floyd persuaded President Buchanan to launch against the Mormons. Brigham Young and his people were making trouble, he argued. They had forced the recall of one federal judge. Another official had been killed. They needed to be taught a lesson.

The offenses hardly justified a $5 million military expedition, but these were strange and unsettled times. Floyd was a Virginian who eventually gave up his post and joined the Confederacy, but only after spiriting some 135,000 firearms and other ordnance from the government arsenal at Springfield, Massachusetts and distributing them through the South and Southwest. It may not be entirely coincidence that he was the one who engineered an expedition to disperse the strongest force of Free-Soilers between the Missouri and Pacific Coast.

The whole affair was at best foolishness, at worst treason, but it was Russell, Majors and Waddell that suffered the most. The company agreed to freight the expedition without the formality of contracts, relying on verbal promises that the Army would make good all losses.

Losses there were, ruinous ones. Tired of running, Brigham vowed the Saints would not be driven out of their mountain refuge. Mormon crews rocked up breastworks in the cliffs above Echo Canyon. Twenty-five hundred men spent much of the winter there, prepared to flood the canyon and roll rocks onto troops below. More breastworks guarded the entrance to the trail up Big Mountain through Little Emigration Canyon.

Those defenses were never used, thanks to far more effective tactics out on the Wyoming plains. Surprising the expedition's advance party in camp on the Green River, Lot Smith and forty-four members of the Nauvoo Legion burned fifty-two wagons carrying 150 tons of food and equipment, and drove hundreds of oxen and beef cattle back

to Utah. Some days later, Porter Rockwell and his troops drove off 900 more oxen that had been rushed up in relief. Unable to move, the army shivered out the winter in Fort Bridger and was later able to enter the valley only by Brigham's negotiated permission.

Because of Young's strict instructions, this strange war cost not a single life. But it cost the government $5 million and nearly bankrupted Russell, Majors and Waddell. Yet, less than three years later, with no promise of government support and knowing there would be heavy losses, that audacious trio launched the Pony Express. Why? Their patriotic conviction that the North badly needed fast, reliable communications with California was probably one reason. Moreover, Russell urged his dubious partners, pulling off such a feat would solidify the company's reputation, ensuring its control of future mail service and, perhaps, even of the coming railroad. Besides, Russell had given his promise to California's Senator Gwin.

That clinched it. Despite what Majors knew about the terrific costs ahead, of warring Indians, snow-filled mountain passes, and scorching deserts, there was no choice. A man's word was his bond.

From the day of decision, the trio gave themselves three months, until April 3, 1860, to put spurs to the first pony. Incredibly, they did it. First, they had to form a new company, the Central Overland and Pike's Peak Express Company. RM&W already owned the stage line from Atchison to Salt Lake City and turned it over to the new company. But the Leavenworth and Pikes's Peak Express

had to be acquired, along with the old Chorpenning mail and stage line that ran monthly between Salt Lake City and Sacramento.

That was the easy part. There was also the task of building stations. The existing stage stations from St. Joseph to Salt Lake would do for home stations, but intermediate relay stations had to be built every ten miles. In the 700 miles from Salt Lake to Sacramento, there was practically nothing; stations had to be built the whole way. Altogether, 190 stations were manned by 400 daring, resourceful men who in their isolation faced the greatest danger of Indian attack.

Then there were the horses—500 of them—some blooded Iowa thoroughbreds, some tough, wiry California cayuses, some wild mustangs rounded up on the Utah desert. Mormon pioneer and scout Howard Egan had the contract to supply ponies for the western sector. Three Mormon teenagers—Ira Nebeker, Sol Hale, and Quince Knowlton—had the job of breaking the wild ones. The horses had to meet two criteria—speed and endurance. The Pony Express was launched at a time of intense Indian hostilities. That only one rider was killed on his ride and one mail lost, despite frequent chases, testifies to the care with which horses were selected.

Recruiting the riders was easier. A famous two-inch advertisement in San Francisco's *Alta California* spelled out first requirements: **Wanted** *Young skinny wiry fellows not over eighteen. Must be expert riders willing to risk death daily. Orphans preferred. Wages $25 per week. Apply, Central Overland Express, Alta Bldg., Montgomery Street.*

There were other requirements. A rider must be sober, God-fearing, and honorable—or at least promise to be. Every man on Majors' payroll had to take this oath of fidelity:

"I _____ , do hereby swear, before the Great and Living God, that during my engagement, and while I am an employe [sic] of Russell, Majors and Waddell, I will, under no circumstances, use profane language; that I will drink no intoxicating liquors; that I will not quarrel or fight with any other employe of the firm, and that in every respect I will conduct myself honestly, be faithful to my duties, and so direct all my acts as to win the confidence of my employers. So help me God."

Whereupon, he was handed a small leather-bound Bible, his red shirt and blue trousers, and sent to his station.

That oath was the same one Majors demanded of all his employes, including the teamsters. Of the latter, Richard Burton on his trip to Utah in 1860 was not much impressed by the result. *"I scarcely ever saw a sober driver,"* he wrote. *"As for profanity—the western equivalent of hard swearing—they would make blush of shame crimson the cheek . . . they are not to be deterred from evil talking even by the dread presence of a 'lady'."*

The Pony Express riders, perhaps because of their tender age, seemed to respond better to Majors' demands for good conduct. Considering the tendency of spirited, green-broke horses to "rodeo" on a frosty morning, however, the oath about profanity may have been occasionally stretched a bit.

Weight-cutting was a priority. Riders were seldom over 125 pounds and they carried only a knife, a pair of revolvers, and—perhaps—the Bible. Combined weight of the saddle and saddle bag, or mochila, was only thirteen pounds. The mochila, with four locked pockets for the mail and with holes for the horn and cantle, was thrown over the entire saddle in such a way that it could be ripped off and thrown onto a new horse in seconds.

And so, through a miracle of organization and efficiency, the system was mostly in place when the target date arrived. On April 3, a cannon boomed in St. Joseph and a black thoroughbred— probably carrying Johnny Frey or Billy Richardson—clattered onto a Missouri River ferryboat, crossed the river, and sped off across the Kansas prairie. At the same hour, the eastbound mail was placed aboard a steamer heading up-river to Sacramento. From there, the first rider, Harry Roff, dashed toward Placerville on a white stallion.

Nine days and twenty-three hours later,

Salsify seedstalks, West Utah Desert
John George

the westbound mail reached Sacramento. Ten days to the minute, the eastbound rider spurred his horse off the ferry and into St. Joseph. The promised ten-day schedule had been met.

Sacramento and San Francisco staged wild celebrations. There was more restraint in Salt Lake City when Howard Egan brought in the first eastbound mail just before midnight on April 7, and when the westbound mail arrived April 10. But the *Deseret News* did manage to opine: *"Although a telegraph is very desirable, we feel well-satisfied with this achievement for the present."* They had good reason to be; the Express brought news from Washington in seven days instead of the accustomed six weeks to three months.

The Pony Express followed the Oregon Trail across Nebraska and Wyoming to South Pass—about the halfway point—and took the California Trail to Fort Bridger. From there,

the ponies followed Donner and Mormon tracks down Echo Canyon to the Weber River, then south up East Canyon, over Big and Little Mountains, and down Emigration Canyon to Salt Lake City.

In a 1979 research project, the Bureau of Land Management identified seven stations, from seven to ten miles apart, from Needle Rock station on the Utah-Wyoming border to Salt Lake City. Nothing remains of any of them, and the precise location of several is uncertain. A stone monument hidden deep in the willows below the Big Mountain highway supposedly marks the location of the Ephraim Hanks [or Mountain Dell] station, but the BLM researchers indicate this may be incorrect. Also challenged is the long-held belief that a station was located at Bauchmann's (now Macfarlane) ranch, where Highway 65 reaches East Canyon Creek.

But if the physical traces are dim, the

romance of what happened here isn't. Heroism was commonplace among the young men who rode the ponies through these mountains. Consider, for example, the ordeal of George Edwin Little, as told by his daughter:

"One day father was bringing in the mail from the east to the station at Mountain Dell. There was a heavy snow storm came up, and crossing over Little [she had to mean Big] *Mountain, the snow became so heavy and deep that his horse gave out and he had to leave him. He took his pocket knife and cut the mail pouches open putting the mail inside his shirt. Then he broke trail over to Mountain Dell, arriving there about 3 o'clock in the morning. The next morning, he rode a horse bareback to Salt Lake and delivered the mail to the Old Salt Lake House which was the home station. Ephraim Hanks, his stepfather, rode back up to the*

canyon next morning and brought in the horse . . . "

The Salt Lake House stood at 143 South Main, at the present site of the Tribune Building. Richard Burton described it in 1860:

"Nearly opposite the Post Office . . . with a long verandah, supported by trimmed and painted posts, was a two-storied, pent-roofed building, whose sign-board, swinging to a tall gibbet-like flagstaff, dressed for the occasion, announced it to be the Salt Lake House, the principal, if not the only establishment of the kind in New Zion. In the Far West, one learns not to expect much of the hostelry; I had not seen aught so grand for many a day." Ruefully, Burton noted that *"We looked vainly for a bar . . . temperance, in public at least, being the order of the day."*

For the Express, there was no stopping at the House. A new rider took the mail here, galloping nine miles south to Travelers Rest station, at State Street and about 60th South, nine more miles to Porter Rockwell's station just below Point of the Mountain, and eleven miles more to Joe's Dugout station, over a pass in the Lake Mountains, just west of the north end of Utah Lake.

This should have been familiar country to the riders, but blizzards and darkness could make it deadly. William Fisher once rode 300 miles in thirty-four hours from Ruby Valley, Nevada, to Salt Lake, bringing word of a Paiute uprising. *"Several stations were burned on the road,"* he recalled, *"and several animals stolen which necessitated my riding so far."* But that heroic ride did not brush death as closely as the night he spent lost and freezing in the Utah Lake/Point of the Mountain country:

"On January 22, 1861, I was lost for 20 hours in a blinding blizzard," he wrote. *"I found myself off the trail up on the hills among the cedar trees. I didn't know where I was, so I just got off my horse and sat down to rest by a thick tree which partly sheltered me from the driving snow. As I sat there holding the reins I began to get drowsy. The snow bank looked like a feather bed, I guess, and I was just about to topple over on it when something jumped on to my legs and scared me. I looked up in time to see a jack rabbit hopping away through the snow. I realized then what was happening to me. If that rabbit hadn't brought me back to my senses I should have frozen right there.*

"I jumped up and began to beat the blood back into my numbed arms and legs. Then I got back on my horse and turned the matter over to him. He wound his way out of the cedars and after about an hour I found myself on the banks of the Jordan River. I knew now where I was so I followed the stream until I came to the bridge that led across to the town of Lehi. When I got there I was nearly frozen to death, but the good woman at the farm house I struck first, filled me with hot coffee and something to eat and I soon felt better.

"When I called for my horse she said, 'You can't get through this storm, better wait till it clears.' 'The mail's got to get through,' I said, and jumped on the pony and struck out, as I thought, for Salt Lake. But as bad luck would have it I wound up about an hour later in front of a deep gulch filled with

snow. I had got this time up into the north-east corner of Utah Valley, near the little town of Alpine, off my trail eight miles. Looking across the gulch I caught sight of a light shining dim through the snow. So I left my horse and plunged down into the gulch and finally made it up the bank to the cabin. When they opened the door I told them of my fix. The man went round and got my horse while I sat thawing out again. By the time he came back the storm had cleared some . . . it was colder than icicles but I could see my way now so I didn't mind. It wasn't long till I reached Rockwell's station by the Point of the Mountain. They gave me a fresh horse and I struck out for Salt Lake on the jump and finally made it home."

Eight miles beyond Dugout, riders reached John Carson's Inn, built in 1858 to serve nearby Camp Floyd. Men like Horace Greeley, Mark Twain, Richard Burton, and General Albert Johnston were among its guests. The handsome two-story adobe building, which still served as an inn as late as 1947, is now a museum operated as the Stagecoach Inn State Park. No other building that served the Pony Express in Utah remains so intact to recall Pony Express and stagecoach days.

Ten miles past the inn was the dugout station at East Rush Valley or Five-Mile Pass. A stone monument marks the spot, and the depression left when the dugout collapsed is still visible.

Nine miles beyond East Rush is Faust Station, first established in 1858 by George Chorpenning, who pioneered this route south of the salt desert for his once-a-month mail service to California. Remains of a stone building still stand; it may have been the original station, but more likely was built a few years later.

H. J. "Doc" Faust operated this station. He had been part of the gold rush to California in 1849, had later joined the Mormon Church and come to Utah, and had spent several years carrying mail to California. A well-educated man, Faust liked to remember the time Horace Greeley stopped at his isolated post, and he saw a great opportunity for conversation with that widely-traveled man. To be certain that Greeley didn't bury himself in a book, Faust hid all the candles. It worked; the conversation, he recalled, was fascinating.

Eight miles from Faust station is Lookout Pass station, from where the whole expanse of desert spreads out to the west. All that remains there is a small cemetery plot, rock-walled and once well-tended. Inside are stone slabs with chiseled names—*"Jenny Lind," "Josephine Bonaparte," "Bishop," "Toby Tyler," "Phoebe"*— names of dogs belonging to Horace Rockwell [Porter's brother] and his wife Libby, who lived here for many years. Nearby—outside the walls—are the unmarked graves of three nameless emigrants.

Local lore has it that Horace Rockwell once paid a man to ride forty miles to Tooele to fetch a doctor and nurse. When Doc Dobbs arrived, he found that the maternity case was not Libby, but Phoebe, who had delivered a fine litter of pups. The house call didn't turn out too well. Phoebe bit Doc, who then prescribed a strong heart stimulant

that Phoebe didn't survive. Doc and the nurse collected their fee and returned to Tooele, and Phoebe now rests in the cemetery.

Just beyond Lookout Pass, the pavement ends—which, of course, dedicated trail- followers welcome. From here through Skull Valley and on to Nevada it's dirt road and empty desert. It's mud or dust, depending on the weather. It's alkali flats and black volcanic hills, shadscale and rabbit brush, and room for imagination unlimited.

Eight miles beyond Lookout is Government Creek, where there logically would have been a relay station. A telegraph station was established on the creek in 1861, but there's no record that the Pony Express was there earlier. No evidence of either remains on the site today.

Simpson Springs, eight miles to the west, became an important Pony Express station and is a major point of interest today. George Chorpenning settled near the spring's excellent water as early as 1851. The stone station house, with portholes for defense and roomy enough to shelter horses inside, was one of the few that escaped burning in Indian attacks. It was at this station that George Perkins found safety and a fresh horse after his desperate 300-mile ride from Ruby Valley, Nevada. It was here, too, that Express rider Nick Wilson was brought, after Indians had ambushed him and buried an arrowhead in his skull. Stationkeeper "Doc" Faust dug out the flint, and, after eighteen days of unconsciousness, Wilson was back on his run.

The BLM has reconstructed the station house about 300 feet east of its original site

A campground and interpretive monument are nearby.

Richard Burton took the Overland Route to San Francisco in 1860 and saw the Pony Express in full operation. He described the country west of Simpson Springs in terms that still fit:

"Standing upon the edge of the bench, I could see . . . the prospect for us . . . a road narrowing in perspective to a point spanned its grisly length, awfully long, and the next mail station had shrunk to a little black knob. All was desert: the bottom could no longer be called basin or valley: it was a thin fine silt, thirsty dust in the dry season, and putty-like mud in the spring and autumnal rains. The hair of this unlovely skin was sage and greasewood: it was warted with sand-heaps; in places mottled with bald and horrid patches of salt soil, whilst in others minute crystals of salt, glistening like diamond-dust in the sunlight, covered tracts of moist and oozy mud . . . "

One man's *"unlovely skin,"* though, may be another man's love. Burton found the West Desert a place to be got through; to rockhounds and trail buffs and solitude-seekers it is one of earth's remaining treasures.

Burton's *"little black knob"* was Riverbed station, eight miles southwest of Simpson Springs and more interesting geologically than historically. During the late stages of Lake Bonneville, water flowed from the south arm of the lake to the north through this narrow gap between two desert mountain ranges. The broad, gravelly channel it cut snakes for miles out into the salt flats. The station was built right in the channel because the ground there was level. Flash floods have long since wiped out any trace of the station.

Not much is known about Dugway station, 10.5 miles from Riverbed, or Blackrock station, fourteen miles beyond that. No one knows the exact location of Blackrock, and only some metal scraps, some piled-up rocks, and an old CCC monument mark the site of Dugway. But there wasn't much there in the first place. As Burton described it:

"It was a mere dugout—a hole four feet deep, roofed over with split cedar trunks, and provided with a rude adobe chimney . . . Three wells have been sunk near the station. Two soon led to rock; the third has descended 120 feet, but is still bone dry." Life could be rough in the desert; every drop of water used at Dugway had to be hauled eighteen miles from Simpson Springs.

Fish Springs, the next station, was another matter. Water was there in such abundance that to reach the station required a wide detour around a southern arm of the salt flats and the marshes that flooded its fringes.

Burton's description is compelling:

"Opposite us and under the western hills, which were distant about two miles, lay the station, but we were compelled to double [detour], for twelve miles, the intervening slough, which no horse can cross without being mired. The road hugged the foot of the hills at the edge of the saleratus basin, which looked like a furrowed field in which snow still lingers. In places warts of earth tufted with greasewood emerged from hard, flakey, curling silt cakes; in others, the salt frosted out of the damp black earth like the miniature sugar-plums upon chocolate bonbons.

" . . . we prepared for the worst part of the stage—the sloughs. These are three in number, one of twenty and the two others of 100 yards in length. The tule, the bayonet-grass, and the tall rushes enable animals to pass safely over the deep slushy muck, but when the vegetation is well trodden down, horses are in danger of being permanently mired. The principal inconvenience to man is the infectious odour of the foul swamps. Our cattle were mad with thirst; however, they crossed the three sloughs successfully, although some had nearly made Dixie's Land [perished] in the second."

Those sloughs, greatly enlarged since Burton's time, are home to countless waterfowl on the Fish Springs National Wildlife Refuge. The rock foundation of the original station is all that remains from Pony Express days. Still, a couple of hours at the refuge is worthwhile, especially in late spring and early summer when young birds are just off the nest. Miles of roads lead past ponds full of great blue herons, snowy egrets, Canada geese, avocets, a dozen species of ducks. No camping is allowed in the refuge, but a BLM campground is nearby.

In good weather, riders climbed a pass over the Fish Springs mountains on a nine-mile trail from Fish Springs to Boyd's station. But that route was too rugged for wagons then, and jeeps can't make it today. In the 1860s, wagons swung around the end of the range, fourteen miles to Boyd's. So does today's road.

Boyd's was a small and not particularly significant station. But because Bid Boyd, the stationmaster, lived there into the twentieth

century, the rock structure is one of the best preserved along the entire Pony Express route. From here, Chorpenning's old mail route turned south to swing around the south end of the Deep Creek Mountains. The Pony Express took a more direct route. It headed straight west eight miles to Willow Springs at Callao.

If there is any inhabited place in Utah where the past is more present than at Callao, I don't know it. Forty-five miles from the nearest pavement, ninety miles from the nearest grocery store, doctor, or movie theater, Callao nestles in its hay-filled valley below the Deep Creek Mountains that soar to the west. Twenty-six people live quiet, peaceful lives there, and it takes some long rides by horseback to assemble the eight kids who make up the kindergarten to eighth grade classes in the one-room school—the only one left in Utah. A pause in Callao and a chat with some of its residents under their towering cottonwood trees is a bonus to any trail-follower.

The trouble is, modern research has muddied the Pony Express waters. The Willow Springs station ought to have been in Callao, on the ranch handed down to David Bagley from his great-grandfather. Folks in Callao have always thought it was, and a stone monument announces that it was. This is the old station house right here, Bagley insists, next to the ranch house and under this round leaf cottonwood tree that botanists have told him is the oldest in the country. It certainly has to be one of the largest; when last officially measured, in 1984, the tree was twenty-six feet three inches around. Bagley is happy

to take visitors inside the old station house and show the small desert- and-Pony Express museum he has assembled there.

But BLM researchers doubt that there was a station on Bagley's ranch. They have located a foundation three-quarters of a mile to the east that they believe more nearly matches descriptions by Burton and others. It is about 100 feet northeast of the adobe-walled F. J. Kearney boarding house, built about the time of the Pony Express and still standing.

Six miles northwest, at Willow Creek, there may have been another station. The evidence for this one is scanty, chiefly a memoir by Express rider Nick Wilson. He remembered:

"Peter Neece, our home station keeper, was a big strong man and a good rider. He was put to breaking some of these wild mustangs for the boys to ride. Generally, just as soon as the hostler could lead them in and out of the stable without getting his head knocked off, they were considered tame, and very likely they had been handled enough to make them mean.

"My home station was Shell Creek [Nevada]. I rode from Shell Creek to Deep Creek [now Ibapah, on the Utah border], and one day the Indians killed the rider out on the desert, and when I was to meet him at Deep Creek, he was not there. I went to the next station, Willow Creek, the first station over the mountain, and there I found out that he had been killed. My horse was about jaded by this time, so I had to stay there to let him rest. I would have had to start back in the night as soon as the horse

got so he could travel, if those Indians had not come upon us. About four o'clock in the afternoon, seven Indians rode up to the station and asked for something to eat. Peter Neece picked up a sack with about twenty pounds of flour in it and offered it to them, but they would not have that little bit, they wanted a sack of flour apiece. Then he threw it back into the house and told them to get out, and that he wouldn't give them a thing. This made them pretty mad, and as they passed a shed about four or five rods from the house, they each shot an arrow into a poor, old lame cow, that was standing under the shed. When Neece saw them do that, it made him mad, too, and he jerked out a couple of pistols and commenced shooting at them. He killed two of the Indians and they fell off their horse there. The others ran. He said 'Now boys, we will have a time of it tonight. There are about thirty of those Indians camped in the canyon there and they will be upon us as soon as it gets dark, and we will have a fight . . . There are four of us and we can stand off the whole bunch of them!'

"Pete thought it would be a good thing to go out a hundred yards or so and lie down in the brush and surprise them as they came up. When we got out there he had us lie down about four or five feet apart. 'Now,' he said, 'when you fire, jump out to one side, so if they shoot at the blaze of your gun, you will not be there.'

"We all took our place, and you bet, I lay close to the ground. Pretty soon we could hear their horses feet striking the ground, and it seemed to me as if there were thous-

Sunset from Fish Springs. Deep Creek Mountains on the horizon.
John George

ands of them, and such yells as they let out, I never heard before. The sounds were coming straight towards us, and I thought they were going to run right over us. It was sandy where we lay, with little humps. Finally the Indians got close enough for us to shoot. Pete shot and jumped to one side. I had two pistols, one in each hand, cocked all ready to pull the trigger, and was crawling on my elbows and knees. Each time he would shoot, I saw him jump. Soon they were all shooting and each time they shot, I would jump. I never shot at all.

"After I had jumped a good many times, I happened to land in a little wash or ravine. I guess my back came pretty nearly level with the top of it. Anyhow, I pressed myself down so I could get in. I don't know how I felt, I was so scared. I lay there and listened until I could hear no more shooting, but I thought I could hear the horses' hoofs beating on the hard ground near me until I found out it was only my heart beating . . .

"Finally everything was very still, so I thought I would go around and see if my horse was where I had staked him, and if he was, I would go back to my station in Deep Creek and tell them that the boys were all killed and I was the only one that had got away. Well, as I went crawling around the house on my elbows and knees, just as easily as I could, with both pistols ready, I saw a light shining between the logs in the back part of the house. I thought the house must be full of Indians, so I decided to lie there a while and see what they were doing. I lay there for some time listening and watching then I heard one of the men speak.

'Did you find anything of him?' Another answered, 'No, I guess he is gone.' Then I knew it was the boys, but I lay there until I heard the door shut, then I slipped up and peeped through the crack and saw that all three of them were there all right.

"I was too much ashamed to go in but finally I went around and opened the door. When I stepped in Pete called out, 'Hello! Here he is. How far did you chase them? I knew you would stay with them. I told the fellows here you would bring back at least half a dozen of them.' I think they killed five Indians that night."

At Canyon, the next station, the result of an encounter with the Indians was less happy, from the whites' point of view. Here, where Overland Canyon snakes down from a spur of the Deep Creek range, Indians hit with total surprise, killing five soldiers and a driver and burning the station. Howard Egan described the attack:

"The Indians waited till the men had been called to breakfast in the dugout, and were all down in the hole without guns, all except the hostler, William Riley, who was currying a horse just outside the south door of the stable at the time of the first alarm, and he was shot through the ankle and the bone broken short off. He started down the canyon on the run, but did not get very far before he was caught and killed.

"The men at breakfast were mostly all killed as they came out of the dugout to reach their arms that were staked in the south end of the barn. Not one of them ever reached his gun. One man, though wounded, tried to escape by running down the canyon

as Riley did. He got further away, but was caught and killed, and, as he was some bald on the top of his head, and a good growth of whiskers on his chin, they scalped that and left him where he fell . . . They took the clothes off every man and left them just where they fell. All this had been done without a shot being fired by the white men."

Another account, by "Doc" Faust, reported that Riley, the hostler, "was only wounded at first; he fought them hard, but was overpowered at last. The Indians tied him, and thrust him on the wood-pile and burned him alive. One of the Indians cut his heart out, and roasted it and ate it, so as to make him brave."

The ruins so prominent today are those of a station relocated in 1863 in a more defensible position and with a round stone fort, complete with gunports—built, obviously, too late.

The last station in what is now Utah was at Ibapah, or Deep Creek. Here, Major Howard Egan had his home ranch, from which he and his sons supplied hay for Pony Express and stage stations for a hundred miles in each direction. Egan had played the major role in scouting out the central mail route. From his ranch he supervised both the Pony Express and the Overland Stage operations from Salt Lake City west through Utah and much of Nevada.

Horace Greeley, passing through in 1859, saw little good in the Deep Creek country. "If Uncle Sam should ever sell that tract for one cent per acre, he will swindle the purchaser outrageously," he reported.

Others saw it differently. Richard Burton

Deep Creek Mountains. Howard Egan managed the western Utah-Nevada segment of the Pony Express from his ranch at the base of these peaks.
John George

wrote in 1860: "*Descending the western watershed, we sighted, in Deep Creek Valley, the first patch of cultivation since leaving Gt. S. Lake. The Indian name is Ayba-pa, or the Clay-coloured Water . . . fields extend about one mile from each bank, and the rest of the yellow bottom is a tapestry of wire grass and wheat grass . . . At 4 p.m. we reached the settlement, consisting of two huts and a station-house, a large and respectable-looking building of unburnt adobe . . . The Mormons were not wanting in kindness they supplied us with excellent potatoes, and told us to make their house our home.*"

Hiram Rumfield, an Overland mail agent, gave a more personal view of life at Deep Creek. Describing Egan's daughter-in-law as "*young . . . beautiful and accomplished*", he continued:

"*They have gathered around them, in this desert region, many of the comforts and some of the refinements of eastern life. While I write, this generous and simple hearted woman is engaged in singing an accompaniment to the tones of the Melodean . . .*"

This is the heart of Pony Express country, scenically as well as historically. Haystack Mountain, the 12,100-foot monarch of the Deep Creek range, broods over the area, 3,000-year-old bristlecone pines clinging to its slopes against the wind. The Gosiute Indian Reservation lies in the western foothills and valleys.

Gosiute legend tells that Mount Ibapah is inhabited by little men who warred with Gosiute ancestors many years ago. A truce was finally called, which gave the Indians the mountain in the daytime but left it to the lit-tle men at night. Indian mothers listening to rock slides on the mountain during the night tell their children that they are caused by the little men playfully rolling rocks down the canyon walls.

In this area, Indians made some of their bloodiest raids on the Pony Express and stage stations. At Eight-mile, the next station west of Deep Creek, the Gosiutes killed one man outright and tortured another to death. As the stagecoach approached, they attacked that, too, shooting the driver and a passenger riding with him. Another passenger managed to climb from the stage interior up to the driver's seat and drive the team in a deadly race to Deep Creek and safety.

That was in 1863. The Pony Express was two years dead. Troops sent from Fort Douglas by General Patrick Conner soon put an end to the Gosiute uprising with slaughter that made little distinction between hostile and peaceful Indians; an entire encampment of Indian families was killed by Conner's soldiers near Simpson Springs while the men were out hunting. With the Indians subdued, stage coaches rolled over the Pony Express route in relative safety for another six years until the joining of the rails in 1869 ended that era forever.

But history has its ironies. When I was last at Eight-Mile Station twenty-five years ago, only the fireplace stood of the Pony Express station house. But the adobe-walled stable where those swift, durable horses had been so carefully housed was still there. Leotta Steele, a Gosiute woman living at the site with her twelve children, was using it as a turkey roost.

*View across Lake Powell to
Hole-in-the-Rock from the top of
Cottonwood Canyon*
Tom Smart

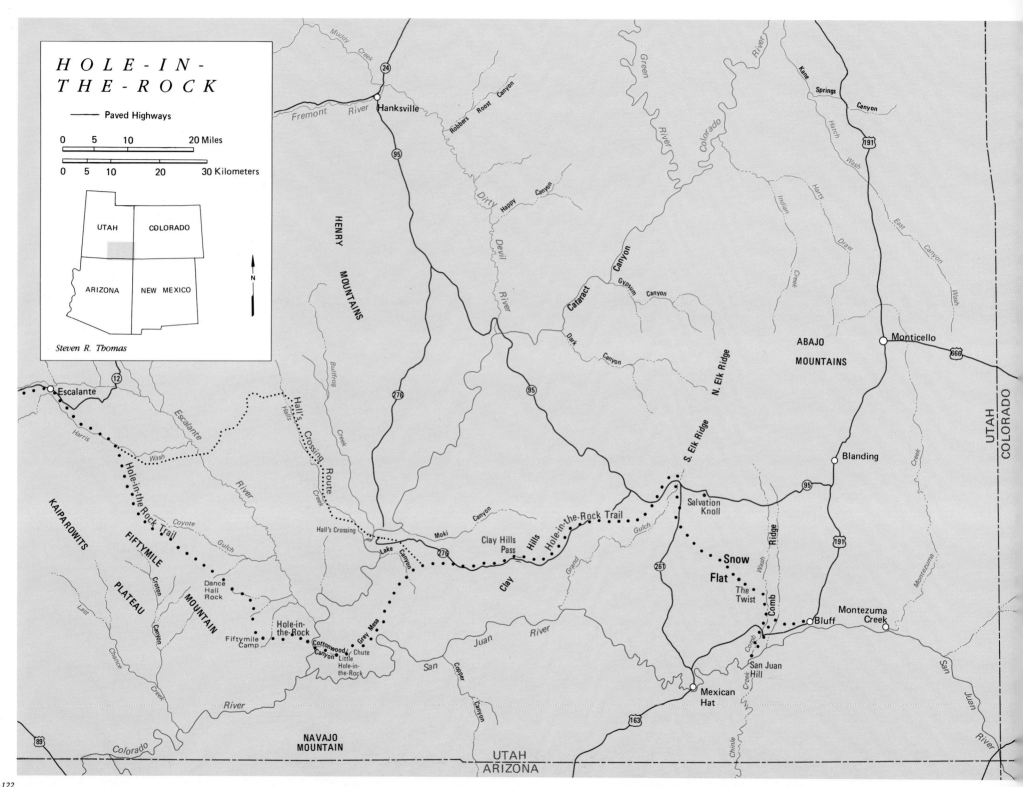

HOLE-IN-
THE-ROCK

Paved Highways

0   5   10   20 Miles

0   5   10   20   30 Kilometers

UTAH   COLORADO

ARIZONA   NEW MEXICO

N

Steven R. Thomas

Muddy Creek

Fremont River

Hanksville

24

95

Robbers Roost Canyon

Green River

Kane Springs

Canyon

191

Dirty Happy Canyon

Devil

River

HENRY

MOUNTAINS

Cataract Canyon

Gypsum Canyon

Dark Canyon

Colorado River

Harts Draw

Indian Creek

East Canyon Wash

ABAJO

MOUNTAINS

Monticello

666

12

Escalante

Harris Wash

Escalante River

Hall's Crossing Route

Halls Creek

Bullfrog Creek

276

95

N. Elk Ridge

S. Elk Ridge

Blanding

95

UTAH

COLORADO

KAIPAROWITS

FIFTYMILE

PLATEAU

MOUNTAIN

Hole-in-the-Rock Trail

Coyote Gulch

River

Dance Hall Rock

Hole-in-the-Rock

Fiftymile Camp

Cottonwood Canyon

Little Hole-in-the-Rock

Chute

Grey Mesa

Hall's Crossing

Moki Canyon

Lake Canyon

276

Clay Hills Pass

Clay Hills

Hole-in-the-Rock Trail

Grand Gulch

Salvation Knoll

Snow

Flat

The Twist

Comb Ridge

261

Bluff

Montezuma Creek

191

Montezuma Creek

San Juan River

Copper Canyon

Wash Ridge

Comb

San Juan Hill

Mexican Hat

163

Chinle Creek

San Juan River

Last Chance Creek

Croton Canyon

Colorado River

NAVAJO MOUNTAIN

UTAH

ARIZONA

89

HOLE-IN-THE-ROCK

It is January 25, 1987. Two hours out of Escalante, we had reached the rim at dusk. With light fading fast, we scatter to find enough of the sparse shadscale for a fire. Soon, with steaks sizzling, water steaming over the Coleman, nylon tents pitched, we can lean back and enjoy the night.

It's cold, but not bitter. Maybe ten or fifteen above zero, snow two or three inches deep, and spotty. Certainly nothing like the numbing cold and deep snow the Hole-in-the-Rock pioneers suffered during the six weeks they labored here to hack and stitch a wagon road from this rim down to the Colorado River and up the other side.

About bedtime, I walk out to the top of the crack, looking down through the hole to Lake Powell, dimly visible in the starlight. And I reflect. How on this night 107 years ago, after working through most of December and January, they had the road ready; they would go down the next day. How sleepless the night must have been, even for men worn thin with labor, with the fearsome prospect of descending that 2,000-foot cliff. How cold it was, so cold that in the days up to and including Christmas no one could work, even when work so desperately needed to be done. Yet, on Christmas night they had built a fire and danced. The children had hung their stockings on wagon wheels and rejoiced next morning that Santa had found them in that desolate place, even though all he had to leave was a little parched corn.

Two hundred fifty men, women, and children were waiting here and in camp a few miles back. With eighty-two wagons and hundreds of head of livestock, they had answered the call of their church to colonize Utah's most remote corner. But first they must go down the Hole.

In the cold early morning, the sky is salmon, a quarter moon and brilliant Venus in the east. First rays of the sun set aflame the rimrock of the Kaiparowits Plateau, the long, unbroken escarpment the pioneers called Fiftymile Mountain because they had trudged below it that far on the road they had carved from Escalante to this place. The Hole is dark, forbidding. So is Cottonwood Canyon, across the lake where they will have to climb out. All around is naked Navajo sandstone frozen into buttes and pinnacles and dunes by 200 million years of time. To the south, above the wilderness of stone looms the splendid laccolithic dome of Navajo Mountain.

At this hour there is total stillness. Not so 107 years ago. The pioneers would have been up in the pre-dawn also; it would be a long day, getting forty wagons down the Hole and as many as possible across the river. There must have been a great din of lowing cattle, neighing horses, jangling harnesses, and creaking wagons, mingling with the cries of excited children and of anxious men giving commands to their teams and each other.

Would the road work? Could a wagon hold together on the dizzying forty-foot drop down the notch they had chiseled through the rimrock? Could it stay upright as it bounced over the precipitous mile of boulders and rubble down to the river? Most worrisome of all, would the road hold on "Uncle Ben's Dugway", where it had been tacked

Kaiparowits Plateau near Fifty-mile Point. The Mormons called the plateau Fiftymile Mountain and followed it from Escalante to the rim of the Colorado.
Fred Hirschmann

for fifty feet along the side of a sheer cliff? Drawing on his Welsh mining background, Benjamin Perkins had engineered that section. Men hanging by ropes in the bitter cold had chiseled out a shelf for the wagons' uphill wheels. Lower, they had drilled a series of holes, a foot and a half apart, in the solid rock face, and into them had driven scrub oak stakes gathered on Fiftymile Mountain. Across the stakes they had laid cottonwood poles hauled up from the river bottom, and on this framework had piled brush and rocks to build a roadbed for the downhill wheels.

It was ingenious, but would it hold? If not, teams, wagons, and people would fall to certain destruction on the rocks below. Because Perkins had designed the dugway, his wagon was given the "honor" of being the first to test it. Wheels were roughlocked. Twenty men clung to ropes and pulled back with all their strength as the wagon tipped over the rim and plunged down the notch. So far so good. Now for the dugway. It held. Uncle Ben's Dugway held for thirty-nine other wagons driven down that day, and for that many more that followed the next day. It even held for two- way traffic in the next few years until a better road was developed with a ferry at Halls Creek.

Of many accounts written of the descent, none is more graphic than one based on the recollections of Joseph Stanford Smith, written by his grandson for *Desert Magazine* (June 1954) and quoted in David E. Miller's excellent book, *Hole in the Rock*. Smith had spent the day in the Hole, helping wagons down. As he climbed out to the rim, he found his wagon, wife and three small children still there, with no men left to help. His story:

"Stanford hooked up the team, two at the tongue and old Nig tied to the rear axle . . . Arabella climbed in and laid the baby on the bed. Stanford started the team toward the crevice through which the wagon must be lowered to the river.

'I'll cross-lock the wheels. Please throw me the chains, Belle.'

She did as he asked, then jumped down to help. Stanford took her arm and they walked to the top of the crevice, where hand in hand they looked down—10 feet of loose sand, then a rocky pitch as steep as the roof of a house and barely as wide as the wagon—below that a dizzy chute down to the landing place, once fairly level but now ploughed up with wheels and hoofs. Below that they could not see, but Stanford knew what was down there—boulders, washouts, dugways like narrow shelves. But it was that first drop of 150 feet that scared him.

'I am afraid we can't make it,' he exclaimed.

'But we've got to make it,' she answered calmly.

They went back to the wagon where Stanford checked the harness, the axles, the tires, the brakes. He looked at Belle, and felt a surge of admiration for this brave, beautiful girl. They had been called to go to San Juan, and they would go. With such a wife, no man could retreat.

'If we only had a few men to hold the wagon back we might make it, Belle.'

'I'll do the holding back,' said Belle, 'on old Nig's lines. Isn't that what he's tied

back there for?'

'Any man with sense in his head wouldn't let a woman do that,' he cried.

'What else is there to do?' she countered.

'But, Belle, the children?'

'They will have to stay up here. We'll come back for them.'

'And if we don't come back?'

'We'll come back. We've got to . . . '

Stanford braced his legs against the dashboard and they started down through Hole-in-the-Rock. The first lurch nearly pulled Belle off her feet. She dug her heels in to hold her balance. Old Nig was thrown to his haunches. Arabella raced after him and the wagon, holding to the lines with desperate strength. Nig rolled to his side and gave a shrill neigh of terror. 'His dead weight will be as good as a live one,' she thought.

Just then her foot caught between two rocks. She kicked it free but lost her balance and went sprawling after old Nig. She was blinded by the sand which streamed after her. She gritted her teeth and hung on to the lines. A jagged rock tore her flesh and hot pain ran up her leg from heel to hip. The wagon struck a huge boulder. The impact jerked her to her feet and flung her against the side of the cliff. The wagon stopped with the team wedged under the tongue. Stanford leaped to the ground and loosened the tugs to free the team, then turned to Arabella. There she stood, her face white against the red sandstone.

He used to tell us she was the most gallant thing he had ever seen as she stood there defiant, blood-smeared, begrimed and, with her eyes flashing, dared him to sympathize.

In a shaky voice he asked, 'How did you make it, Belle?'

'Oh, I crow-hopped right along!' she answered. He looked away.

He walked to the apparently lifeless form of Nig, felt his flank. It quivered under his hand and Nig tried to raise his bruised and battered head.

Stanford then looked up the crack. Up there on the sharp rocks a hundred feet above him waved a piece of white cloth, a piece of her garment. Why, she had been dragged all that way.!

'Looks like you lost your handkerchief, Belle.' He tried to force a laugh, instead choked and grabbed her to him, his eyes going swiftly over her. A trickle of blood ran down her leg, making a pool on the rocks. 'Belle, you're hurt! And we're alone here.'

'Old Nig dragged me all the way down,' she admitted.

'Is your leg broken?' he faltered.

She wouldn't have his sympathy; not just yet, anyway. 'Does that feel like it's broken?' she fairly screamed, and kicked his shin with fury.

He felt like shaking her, but her chin began quivering and he had to grin, knowing by her temper she wasn't too badly hurt. He put his arms around her and both began crying, then laughing with relief.

They had done it! Had taken the last wagon down—alone.''

I thought of Stanford and Belle and old Nig as I picked my way down the Hole on the anniversary of their ordeal. Above, great icicles, loosened by the sun, broke away from the cliff face and crashed on the rocks around us. Did the pioneers face that hazard, too? No accounts mention it.

Only the chiseled shelf and the stake holes remain of Uncle Ben's Dugway. Mammoth boulders block the bottom of the gorge; the rocks and dirt with which the pioneers so laboriously covered them have eroded away. The bottom third of the road is covered by Lake Powell. Much has changed over those 107 years, but climbing up the Hole, as thousands have done from their boats on Lake Powell, still fills one with wonder at what those pioneers did here—and why?

What was going on here? Trails are supposed to follow the best compromise between shortest distance and easiest terrain.

But these people had forced a ridiculously impossible trail down to the Colorado. And worse lay ahead. To climb out of the river, up Cottonwood Canyon, would require roadbuilding, including more dugways like Uncle Ben's, almost as difficult as that down the Hole. Their own scouts had reported that the savage slickrock maze east from the river was utterly impassable for wagons. And 120 miles of heartbreaking labor still lay between them and their proposed home on the San Juan.

What could have brought sensible men and women to such a place?

By the late 1870s, Mormon colonization of Utah was mostly complete. Colonies had reached out as far as San Bernardino, California; Carson Valley, Nevada; Fort Lemhi on the Salmon River in Idaho, and the Little Colorado in Arizona—though some had since been pulled back.

But one part of Utah knew no settlement, Mormon or otherwise—the vast slickrock canyon wilderness east and south of the Colorado River. This Colorado Plateau country, today a magnet for backpackers, river runners, and four-wheelers, was then unex-

plored. The first relief map published of Utah, in Dutton's 1879 *Atlas of the High Plateaus*, shows the southeast corner of Utah virtually blank. The only inhabitants were Indians and a few outlaws who occasionally hid out in the deep canyons.

To bring law and order to the region, to act as a buffer against cattle-raiding Indians, and to claim the country against cattlemen and miners who were beginning to push in from Colorado and New Mexico, Brigham Young decided to establish a settlement in this rugged country. His death in 1877 caused delays, but by late 1878 plans were firming. A call from the pulpit at stake conference in Parowan on December 28 named forty-eight adult males to the colonizing mission. Others were called in March at Cedar City. Still others came, as volunteers or as called missionaries, from most of the then-organized counties south of Provo.

A thirty-strong advance expedition left Paragonah on April 14, 1879, to explore and rough out a wagon road, locate suitable lands for settlement, file claims, put in crops, and build houses. They headed south into Arizona, then east to cross the Colorado at Lees Ferry, pushed on south to Moenkopi, then turned northeast to reach the San Juan on May 30 near present-day Montezuma. They spent ten weeks there exploring the country, filed on all likely-looking land, built a dam and irrigation ditches, and planted crops that later would wither and die as the river dropped. Two families remained to wait for the main group, which was expected to arrive before the year was out.

But the explorers decided that the southern route was too dry and too rough for a larger expedition. Too many wells would have to be dug and too much road built. Besides, after a few clashes with the Indians, they concluded that taking a large company with hundreds of livestock through Navajo country would not be healthy. So they returned by a northern route, basically following the Old Spanish Trail. The report, when they reached Paragonah in mid-September after a 1,000-mile roundtrip, was that the San Juan was nice country to settle, but a better way would have to be found to get there.

The "better way" became the shortcut by way of the town of Escalante and Hole-in-the-Rock. How it could have been chosen is hard to comprehend. But the southern route was reported as impractical, and the northern route meant 250 extra miles of travel. Besides, Andrew Schow, bishop of Escalante, and Reuben Collett, the town constable, had been assigned to scout out the shortcut. They had hauled a two-wheel cart to the Colorado rim, had worked it down the cliffs to the river, floated it across, and explored two or three miles up Cottonwood Canyon on the other side. Getting wagons down the cliffs would be difficult but could be done, they reported. Once across the river, a good road could be made *"through the country beyond to the San Juan River."*

But the two men had not seen the country beyond, only the easy going in the bottom of Cottonwood Canyon. Had they climbed to the head of that canyon, they would have found it boxed in by naked sandstone cliffs that could only be conquered by the same kind of road work done at the Hole. Had they climbed to the top and on up to Grey Mesa they would have found themselves in the wildest, most challenging country I have seen in half a lifetime of four-

View across slickrock wilderness to Grey Mesa, one of the most formidable barriers on the Hole-in-the-Rock trail. Navajo Mountain in distance.
John George

wheeling. Those who have not seen this region—and very few have—can imagine its difficulty from the fact that after a second and more extensive exploration, the same experienced men who had thought it perfectly feasible to hack a road down Hole-in-the-Rock brought back a report that building a wagon road through this country would be impossible.

But by the time the pioneers heard that negative report they had already spent a month building a road forty miles across the desert southeast from Escalante. It was December. Snow had come early and deep on the Wasatch Plateau that lay between them and their homes. It would be impossible, they thought, to return until spring, and the tiny settlement at Escalante could not support them and their herds through the winter. Besides, they were Mormons, and they trusted their leaders. Where was the faith of those who talked of impossibilities?

At Forty-mile Spring on December 3, the leaders heard the scouts' majority report; they could not go forward. But there was a minority report by George Hobbs, one of the scouts, endorsed by Schow and Collett; with faith and effort, the road could be built. The decision was made, and endorsed with remarkable unity by the entire company the next day: the trek would go forward. The dancing at nearby Dance Hall Rock must have reflected a special spirit that night.

Today's graded road from Escalante to Dance Hall Rock and on to Fifty-mile Spring closely follows the old wagon road except where it crosses washes—Harris, Coyote, Hurricane—draining into the Escalante River.

At those places, modern road builders had to follow easier grades than the steep pitches negotiated by the pioneers, whose rock work is still visible in spots. Today's road is dusty when dry, slippery when wet, and occasionally treacherous. Some years ago we spent half a day digging a four-wheel-drive outfit out of quicksand left in the road by a flash flood.

From Forty-mile Spring to Fifty-mile Spring, where most of the pioneers stayed while the Hole was blasted out, and on to the Hole itself, the road nearly loses itself in naked slickrock and shifting sand. With great care and in dry weather, a passenger car can negotiate it, but it is not recommended. In his remarkable daily journal of the trek, Platte D. Lyman, the leader, described this section as *"the roughest white men ever undertook to pass over."* He had seen nothing yet.

From Lake Powell, boaters can hike up Cottonwood Canyon, where the pioneers climbed out after dropping down the Hole and ferrying across the river. Deep underwater is Register Rock, where many of the pioneers carved their names. Also flooded is the campsite, four miles from the river, where the company stayed during a week of heroic labor finishing a road up the solid sandstone cliffs that guard the head of the canyon.

Much work had been done here during the weeks of labor at the Hole. There had been little blasting powder then; it was all pick and shovel and crowbar. But as the main company arrived in Cottonwood Canyon, so did 1,000 pounds of powder from the settlements. Now the work could really move.

The first obstacle was a steep 100-yard sand

dune. Doubling teams, they struggled up, wagons sinking to their axles in the soft, shifting sand, men leaning against ropes on the uphill side to keep from capsizing. Next, they had to tackle the two 500-foot cliffs, one above the other, that blocked the way. Armed with knowledge gained at the Hole, the pioneers broke through this immense obstacle in remarkable time. The product of their work is still plainly visible—shelves dug out for upper wheels of wagons, rocks piled masonry-fashion to support the lower wheels. Uncle Ben's Dugway was repeated here, and the holes and remnants of the stakes are still in place. Large sections of rock were blasted away.

Even so, it was a cruelly steep and risky climb, especially the last section, which even after cutting and blasting was still so narrow they called it "Little Hole in the Rock." Platte Lyman recorded that it took four to seven span of horses or oxen to haul each wagon to the top. Three months later, on a trip bringing new supplies to the infant settlement on the San Juan, Lyman's wagon overturned here, *"breaking the reach, box, bows, flour sacks and some other things and scattered my load all over the side of the hill."* Some have called it Platte Lyman Hill ever since.

In a letter written on the trek, Elizabeth Decker described the country beyond Cottonwood Hill: *"It's the roughest country you or anybody else ever seen; it's nothing in the world but rocks and holes, hills and hollows. The mountains are just one solid rock as smooth as an apple."*

To see that country today takes a sound horse or a good pair of legs and plenty of time. Or it takes two or more short-wheel-based, winch-equipped jeeps, steady nerves, a touch of foolhardiness, and someone who knows the trail. Someone like Lynn Lyman. Now in his eighties and a lifelong resident of Blanding, he has trucked and four-wheeled through southeast Utah's slickrock country since he was a teenager. His father was a Hole-in-the-Rock pioneer; his uncle was the leader. The trail is in his blood. No one has spent more time on it or has known it better.

Jeeping this section with someone like Lynn is a climax experience. Up and down slickrock so steep you swear the vehicle will somersault forward, or backward; across side-hills where it can't possibly remain upright, but does; through bottomless sand pockets, up and down incredibly rough dugways where you prop up your wheels with what may be the same boulders the pioneers used to prop up theirs.

"Isn't this the roughest country you've ever driven through?" an awestruck passenger asks Lyman as he tries to pick a way into the redrock wilderness of Wilson Canyon.

"Yes, it is. Especially when you're hopelessly lost . . . like I am now."

He was, too. Shortly, the jeep ground to a halt at the brink of a 400-foot cliff.

"One thing about going that way," he chuckled. *"It'd be quicker."*

But Lynn Lyman doesn't stay lost long in this country. He's long since lost count of the number of trips he's made out here to show others the trail, but he guesses it's around fifty. He's concerned that when he's gone his knowledge of the trail will go with him. With

him as a guide, the Utah Historical Society, Bureau of Land Management, Boy Scouts of America, and San Juan County officials launched in 1987 a project of marking the trail so future generations will know exactly where it went.

One place that needs no marking is the Chute, the only way out of Wilson Canyon. This famous landmark is an impossibly steep ravine of smooth, naked rock. Chutes are everywhere in slickrock country, where flashflood waters have eroded paths from jump pool to jump pool. Most of them are a few feet long, a foot or two wide. This one out of Wilson Canyon is 100 yards long, ten feet wide, and scary. The pioneers climbed it by doubling teams and hauling in rocks to improve the footing. Modern four-wheelers creep up in low-low gear, leaving plenty of burnt rubber on the rock.

The first white men to travel through this impossible country were four scouts, George Hobbs, L. H. Redd, George Morrill and George Sevy, sent to explore from the Hole all the way to the San Juan to see what really lay ahead. With four mules and two horses, they managed to get up Cottonwood Hill, through the incredible jumble of naked rock and impassable canyons beyond, and onto Grey Mesa, about ten miles from the river. But in hours of searching they could find no way off the mesa. Redd's son, James, a teenager with the expedition, later described how the company was saved from failure:

"They crossed the river went up to the slick rock and prospected from one river to the other [the Colorado to the San Juan; this country is a triangle between the junction of

the two] *and decided just as the other party* [the second group of explorers] *had decided that the country could not be crossed. They camped that night and were packing up the next morning to go back to the main company to report their findings when eight mountain sheep came into camp which were so gentle that they would not move away from the party. No one in the party had a gun, and the only rope they had was the pack ropes on the mules. George Hobbs unpacked a mule, secured a rope and attempted to rope a sheep but it eluded him by keeping just out of the way. He followed the sheep until it reached the rim of the canyon where the sheep [climbed over] a shelf and rimmed around from shelf to shelf until it reached the bottom of the ledge. Hobbs followed the sheep for about two hours and the other men had begun to get worried about him. Finally they heard him call, 'Boys, I have found a road.' "*

Getting the wagons later down that sheep track to the valley floor 1,000 feet below took another exhausting week of cutting dugways through solid rock from ledge to ledge. While they were doing it, Mons Larson and his twenty-three-year-old wife, Olivia, reached the top of the mesa in a blizzard. On the climb up, Olivia had carried a two-and-a-half-year-old child under one arm and a one-and-a-half-year-old under the other, just as she had carried them down the Hole. The childrens' feet had been frost-bitten in the bitter cold, and the parents spent most of the night doctoring them.

The next day, February 21, lying in the wagon seat while her husband struggled to

The Hole-in-the-Rock from Lake Powell
Charles Kay

129

pitch a tent against the raging blizzard, Olivia delivered her third child, a healthy boy. At this spot, the San Juan River swings in a great bend against the cliffs 1,000 feet straight down. So, they named the baby John Rio.

In characteristic understatement, the pioneers called this section where they built a road off Grey Mesa the Slick Rocks. It is one of the most poignantly moving places on the trail. Drill holes for sidehill dugways are still there, the stakes still in place. Deep gouges in the sandstone testify to the desperate struggle of shod horses and oxen to keep their footing. Hub-high gouges and rust stains mark the stone where wagons squeezed through.

No jeep has ever been able to negotiate the Slick Rocks. It is Lynn Lyman's priceless legacy to history that none ever will. In the 1950s, an oil exploration company mobilized its bulldozers and dynamiters to gouge a road onto Grey Mesa by the pioneers' route. Lyman heard about it, scouted out an alternate route, and persuaded the company to use it instead. The oil road, barely manageable by four-wheelers, is the only way a jeep can reach the top of Grey Mesa and the *"roughest country you or anyone else ever seen"* between it and the head of Cottonwood Canyon.

From the bottom of the Slick Rocks, the pioneers bounced across eight miles of rocky valley floor to reach Pagharit [or Hermit] Lake near the head of Lake Canyon on February 29. Platte Lyman described the lake as *"a beautiful clear sheet of spring water 1/2 mile long and nearly as wide, and apparently very deep. Cottonwood, willow, canes, flags,*

bulrushes and several kinds of grass grow luxuriantly, and it would make an excellent stock ranch." A bath here must have been a welcome relief after a month of laboring over slickrock with only waterpockets to slake the thirst of livestock and people. The company rested at the lake for two days, washing clothes and recruiting their livestock, before crossing the natural dam and pushing on.

Lake Pagharit today is only a memory. In 1915, a flash flood breached the dam and scoured the canyon bare. With the dam gone, there is no way to follow the old trail across the canyon. Modern explorers must backtrack to a rough jeep road through sand washes and tamarisk around the head of Lake Canyon and rejoin the trail on the shadscale flats south of the Halls Crossing highway.

On level ground at last, the pioneers found easy going for fifteen miles, along the present route of Highway 276, to Clay Hill Pass. But the land falls off a thousand feet from the pass to Whirlwind Bench, and the road-builders went to work again, this time hacking through sticky blue clay rather than solid rock. It took a week to build this section of road, evidences of which can be seen, angling down a steep, rough sidehill north of the highway and then crossing and plunging down a rocky wash to the southeast.

The pioneers reached the bottom of this obstacle on March 13 and found themselves in a blizzard, shivering from the bitter cold. Lyman wrote: *"Last night was the coldest night I ever experienced, it was impossible to be comfortable in bed or anywhere else."*

To the east, they could see where the long, straight-sided, and impassable cliffs of

Comb Ridge fall off to the San Juan River. Just beyond, not more than sixty crow-flight miles away, was their destination. How they must have ached to get there. The trek that was to have taken six weeks had already lasted four months. Teams and people were giving out. And the San Juan was so close.

But they were not crows and could not fly over the awesome gorge slashed by the Grand Gulch all the way from Elk Mountain to the San Juan. So, following the trail blazed weeks earlier by the four scouts, the company turned northeast to circle the head of the Gulch. Their route closely parallels present-day Highways 276 and 95 and a few miles of 261.

The going was easier here, though the labor of breaking through slickrock was replaced by that of slogging through axle-deep mud and, as the trail climbed higher, snow. It was in this country, near the head of Grand Gulch, that the four scouts, lost and not knowing which way to go, had eaten their last scrap of food. They would not have another bite for three days. George Hobbs later wrote:

"It was Christmas day, 1879, which found us on the side of the Elk Mountain without food, in the midst of a piercing cold, and not a mountain in sight that I could recognize. I was the only member of the party that had been to Ft. Montezuma [the destination of the exploring party the previous spring]. *It surely looked like our bones would bleach not far from that point, as it was impossible for us to retrace our steps to our river camp, and not knowing which way to go to reach our destination on the San Juan . . . Seeing*

a small mound to the south I climbed it to see if I could see any further. This was surely Salvation Knoll, for on looking to the northeast across a spur of the Elk Mountain I discovered the Blue [Abajo] *Mountains, about 10* [actually about 25] *miles away."*

The "small mound" is just south of Highway 95, a mile west of Mule Canyon ruins. Today, it is a steep, scrambling hike to the top of Salvation Knoll. But considering what Hobbs had been through, his description is understandable.

The pioneer journals have little to say about the sixteen days spent swinging around the head of Grand Gulch and down to Comb Wash. The teams were nearing exhaustion and struggled in the mud and snow. Chopping crews worked ahead of the wagons, clearing a road through the heavy pinyon-juniper forest. If they were aware of the great natural bridges they passed a mile or two away, which later became a national monument, they made no mention of it. Nor is there any reference to the Anasazi dwellings and rock art in Grand Gulch itself. Perhaps their exhaustion made them oblivious to anything other than the task of getting through this exasperating country.

A fascinating section of trail for modern explorers takes off to the east from Highway 261 about seven miles south of the Kane Gulch ranger station. The old road winds for ten miles through the dense cedars, into and out of washes, challenging but negotiable to the four-wheeler. Ancient stumps in the middle of the trail show where the ax-wielders did their work. In many places, new trees grow between the wagon tracks. Indians cut

firewood and gather pine nuts here. Some careful jeeping over unmarked slickrock to the edge of one side canyon ends with a hike to the finest Anasazi dwelling in its original state I have found in thirty years of searching them out.

The road emerges from the cedars onto Snow Flat, angles down through the rocky ledges that the pioneers named The Twist, and, finally, into Comb Wash. There's no way to cross the long line of 1,000-foot perpendicular cliffs known as Comb Ridge. But no matter. Ten miles down the wash to the San Juan River—not so easy with jaded teams in the deep, loose sand—then around the end of the Ridge, along the river, and home, they thought, would be virtually in sight.

But this harsh country had one more cruel surprise. There is no way along the river. Ledges of naked rock plunging to river's edge block the way.

The only way is up the nose of the Ridge itself. But it's so long—a mile, at least. And so steep. So ledgy, and sidling. Think of the pick work it's going to take, the dugways to be hacked out, the rock masonry to be built on the steep sidehills. Can people as worn as these do that? And if they do, can the gaunt, feeble horses and oxen that have hauled wagons up so many impossible places do it this one more time?

They can and they do, at terrible cost. In his moving account, *Shortcut to San Juan*, Charles Redd described the ordeal:

"Aside from the Hole-in-the-Rock itself, this was the steepest crossing on the journey [not quite true, but to the exhausted party

it must have seemed so. Certainly it was the longest stretch of such steepness]. *Here again seven span of horses were used, so that when some of the horses were on their knees fighting to get up to find a foothold, the still-erect horses could plunge upward against the sharp grade. On the worst slopes the men were forced to beat their jaded animals into giving all they had. After several pulls, rests, and pulls, many of the horses took to spasms and near-convulsions, so exhausted were they. By the time most of the outfits were across, the worst stretches could easily be identified by the dried blood and matted hair from the forelegs of the struggling teams. My father* [L. H. Redd, Jr.] *was a strong man, and reluctant to display emotion; but whenever in later years the full pathos of San Juan Hill was recalled either by himself or by someone else, the memory of such bitter struggles was too much for him and he wept."*

Hiking up San Juan Hill, I thought of Olivia Mons, who carried her two babies up Grey Mesa and there, in a blizzard, delivered a third. And of Anna Decker, who delivered her third child, Lena Deseret Decker, in the bitter January cold of Fifty-mile Camp. How did such women as these, and others with the care of tiny children, still have the strength to carry them up this last long hill?

There are certain places on the Hole-in-the-Rock trail with a special feeling of heroism and sacrifice. One is the Hole itself, seen in comfort by thousands of boaters every year. Less known and seldom seen are Cottonwood Hill, the Chute, the Slick Rocks. Another is Salvation Knoll, unmarked and

known to few. But no place on the trail is more hallowed than one two-thirds up San Juan Hill, where there was still terribly hard pulling ahead but the worst was over and the pioneers knew they were going to make it.

There, under an overhanging ledge to the right of the trail, someone carved in the rock four simple words:

Thanks be to God

Now remained only a short but difficult climb into and out of Butler Wash a couple of miles north of present-day Highway 163 before rolling out into the sandy, blessedly level meadows along the San Juan. Eighteen more miles, a day's travel along easy river bottoms, and they would reach Montezuma Creek, their designated home. But they would never travel those eighteen miles. Six months of grinding labor were enough. They were too tired. This place, Bluff, would be their home.

Epilogue. That 250 men, women and children, eighty-two wagons, and hundreds of head of livestock could have made the trek without loss of human life or even serious accident astonishes anyone who dares the trail today. But they did, through an abundance of the experience, care, and cooperation that successful pioneering demands. Calling on those same qualities, they laid out the town of Bluff, built their homes, planted their crops.

But it was all wrong. The land was too limited, the soil too thin, the San Juan River either too high or too low for irrigation. The town never prospered. Gradually, the pioneers who remained died off. Their descendants moved away.

In the barren, rocky cemetery on the hill

above town lie many of the pioneers who dared all and sacrificed so much to drive the stakes of Zion on the San Juan. Platte Lyman, the practical, capable leader, is buried here, his wife beside him. Here is Roswell Stevens, at seventy-one the first to die in Bluff, a month after the trek ended. The Perkins and the Bartons, the Powells, the Adairs, the Hunts, the Redds, all are here. So is Amassa Barton, murdered by Indians in his trading post at the foot of San Juan Hill. Here is Jens Nielson, and his wives, Else and Kirsten. All had starved and frozen through the handcart tragedy of 1856, yet had willingly answered the San Juan Mission call twenty-three years later. Jens, who described the "Hole" trek as by far the worst of the two, was sixty years old when he reached the San Juan; he remained there as bishop for twenty-five years.

What sorrow he and others who sacrificed so dearly to establish this place would feel if they could know that not a single descendant of a Hole-in-the-Rock pioneer lives in Bluff today. The church for which they gave everything barely exists there; officials have to come from Blanding to conduct services.

But Bluff now prospers, in its own way. Red rocks and running water and desert quiet attract people that farming never could. The "outsiders" the San Juan pioneers were sent to forestall have come anyway, a century later. Artists, writers, photographers, geologists, mining engineers, river guides, and lodge operators have bought and restored the handsome sandstone homes built by the pioneers. It is ironic that these are the people who are keeping Bluff's physical heritage alive.

Sons and daughters of Hole-in-the-Rock pioneers at annual reunion in Cottonwood Canyon. Left to right: Arthur Adair, Alma Jones, Lynn Lyman, Margaret Lyman Jones, Mildred Butt Posey.
William B. Smart

Graves of Hole-in-the-Rock pioneers in the windswept cemetery above Bluff, Utah. No descendant now lives in the town they founded.
Tom Smart

AUTHOR

Author at carved inscription on San Juan Hill. Near the end of the six-month ordeal, an unknown pioneer carved, "We Thank Thee Oh God."
William B. Smart

During his forty years at the *Deseret News*, fourteen as editor and general manager, Bill Smart spent much of his spare time hiking, skiing, and jeeping Utah's back country and exploring its historic trails. He has traveled and written about the world from the South Pole to the glaciers of Alaska, from the Andean Altiplano to Himalayan base camps, from the Berlin Wall to the Great Wall, from the Khyber Pass to the gorges of the Yangtze. But ask him about his favorite place on earth and you'll likely hear more about Utah's red rock country than you want to know.

Near Bluff, Utah
John George